Effective Classroom Turnaround

Practice Makes Permanent

John Jensen

ROWMAN & LITTLEFIELD EDUCATION
A division of
ROWMAN & LITTLEFIELD PUBLISHERS, INC.
Lanham • New York • Toronto • Plymouth, UK

Published by Rowman & Littlefield Education
A division of Rowman & Littlefield Publishers, Inc.
A wholly owned subsidiary of The Rowman & Littlefield Publishing Group, Inc.
4501 Forbes Boulevard, Suite 200, Lanham, Maryland 20706
www.rowman.com

10 Thornbury Road, Plymouth PL6 7PP, United Kingdom

British Library Cataloguing in Publication Information Available

Library of Congress Cataloging-in-Publication Data

Jensen, John, 1935-
Effective classroom turnaround : practice makes permanent / John Jensen.
p. cm.
Includes bibliographical references and index.
ISBN 978-1-4758-0097-5 (cloth : alk. paper) -- ISBN 978-1-4758-0098-2 (pbk. : alk. paper) -- ISBN 978-1-4758-0099-9 (electronic)
1. Classroom management. 2. Effective teaching. 3. Motivation in education. I. Title.
LB3013.J46 2012
371.102'4--dc23
2012022259

The paper used in this publication meets the minimum requirements of American National Standard for Information Sciences Permanence of Paper for Printed Library Materials, ANSI/NISO Z39.48-1992.

Printed in the United States of America

Contents

Other Titles in the *Practice Makes Permanent* Series

Teaching Students to Work Harder and Enjoy It: Practice Makes Permanent

Changing Attitudes and Behavior: Practice Makes Permanent

Preface

How do you nail a piece of learning?

The context is sports, as in nailing a three-point basket or a vault dismount. Implied are a vital moment, a special effort, and a demonstration of excellence that leaves no doubt. In school, we watch a kindergarten teacher nailing learning on the first day of school.

"When you're on the playground and the bell rings, you form a line at the door. Now, what do you do when the bell rings?" They all answer together, "We form a line at the door."

The teacher congratulates them, and in a box on the board writes "1." She tells them, "You just learned one thing. Wasn't that easy? That's what we're going to do every day. We're going to learn lots of easy things and count them up. Now what was it, again, that you do when the bell rings?"

They answer, "Line up at the door!"

"One more time," she says, "and louder."

"Line up at the door!" they shout.

Now they own that piece of knowledge and proceed to rules for the classroom and onward into their lifetime of knowledge: get this point, own it, get another, own it, and so on. The score written in the box on the board is like a deed to a piece of ground, a claim that this chunk is theirs for good. Minute by minute, they nail pieces of learning and feel invigorated. Their vital moment is the teacher's challenging question, their special effort is to listen, their demonstration is to answer firmly, and the result is pleasure at success.

Repeating a single behavior like that, of course, would be like basketball as only a free throw contest. Interest lies instead in the many ways to demonstrate excellence—a tomahawk dunk, a perfectly executed fast break, an agile block, or a crucial jump shot.

Back in the classroom, how do students obtain the same sense of challenge, special effort, and achievement? How does nailing their learning guide their effort? How do we make learning firm enough to satisfy any test yet with the emotional flavor of a three-point shot in the closing seconds of a basketball game?

The few essential conditions are familiar:

1. Skill development of any kind depends on practice.
2. Feelings and communications affect learning.
3. Students need to know where to place their effort.
4. They need increments of success and reinforcement for them.
5. They develop comprehensive knowledge by assimilating it piece by piece.

Nothing startling here, but some ways of doing those simple things stimulate students by engaging their energy quickly. You don't need a district reorganization to know. In a few days you say, "This interests them. They sit up and take notice, and they're learning."

I have seen the ideas explained here succeed from kindergarten through high school, and with the most difficult students any teacher is likely to encounter: students who have severe emotional and behavioral disabilities, middle and high school students bounced from the public system, and elementary classes coming apart.

Yet there is no need to take anyone's word. The methods work in a couple weeks, and you can observe their effects directly without financial outlay or a new curriculum. Use them with what you already teach, and watch students learn and feel better. We confine the focus here to the ordinary tasks in one room, hour by hour between teacher and students.

This book is third in the Practice Makes Permanent series. The first was Teaching Students to Work Harder and Enjoy It: Practice Makes Permanent, and the second, Changing Attitudes and Behavior: Practice Makes Permanent. Each contains the essentials of the approach but with its own emphasis. This one is a concise explanation of how to carry out key methods in addition to numerous approaches not mentioned in the prior books.

Chapter 1 begins with the pilot program that initiated the design. Chapters 2 to 8 describe the methods in detail and are arranged in several categories. The first set offers nine quick-start methods that comprise the basic structure for success and good feelings. Chapters 3 and 4 show how to develop refined communications and aid students' emotional self-management. Chapters 5 to 8 explain how to practice learning to generate permanent retention, ways to think about designing a curriculum and focusing student effort, how scoring instead of grading can solve the problem of assessing student learning, and ways students can demonstrate their learning. Implementation, appendices, and references conclude the book.

Depending on the context, the use of "we" may mean "you and I," "we humans," or "those who work in classrooms." If the meaning is clear, I stay with terms in general use over those with specialized meaning in education. Sub-numbering within sections generally is to unify a set or sequence. Parenthetical numbers preceded by cf. refer the reader one of the fifty-four methods. Capitalization of a method within a paragraph indicates that it is explained in more detail elsewhere.

John Jensen
April 2012

Chapter One

An Epiphany

A clue about how to arouse energy for learning came in the early 1990s.

On a Saturday afternoon when my son was in middle school, I watched him and his friends dash about a rain-soaked field in a soccer game. They were motivated, yet almost all were indifferent students. I could imagine them walking into school through an invisible force field that zapped their wits.

Why was the playing field so different? Participants were the same, so it had to be the dynamics. On the field, twenty-two boys were motivated, executing tiring maneuvers under unpleasant conditions, but they demonstrated skill, scored to validate their effort, linked effort to results, had team support, performed publicly, and practiced to improve. A few guidelines unlocked enormous energy. Where, I wondered, was the pocket rule book showing how to do the same in classrooms?

I put together an outline of methods and called 150 schools in the Seattle area. A few let me speak to teacher meetings. Finally, the African-American Academy staff gave me ten minutes, after which I offered my services free of charge. There was a pause.

"I'd like to point out," said the principal, Dr. Joe Drake, "that the price is right."

Afterward, Leonard Dawson Jr., a fourth grade teacher, caught me. "When can you come to my classroom?" he asked.

In explaining his situation, he felt confident, he said, of his ability to get academics across, but the problem lay in the students' attitude. The previous teacher had been unable to keep order and the students had "run her off."

"They were hostile and aggressive to her and each other," he said and described several unhappy incidents. "They don't understand how to get along. They fight a lot and they make really hurtful comments. Someone might say 'If you look at me again like that, I'll kill you,' and they mean it. By the force of my effort, I'm able to keep order and make some headway in learning. But the minute I let up, things just disintegrate."

The next morning, his students eyed me suspiciously.

"Dr. Jensen is here to help us learn how to get along better," Mr. Dawson told them. "Would you please give us your attention?"

We began with a simple exercise of naming a feeling. He called on each student and asked, "What are you feeling today? Can you give just one word about what you're feeling?" A brief personal word from everyone got their attention and hinted that they would be the focus.

He offered the question to each of the twenty-six students and then went around a second time inviting them to tell what specifically gave them the feeling. They cooperated in a guarded manner with one-word answers. Then we began a remembering exercise, dividing the group into pairs and selecting a topic together. We asked the speakers to talk for two minutes and then for listeners to summarize as much as they could remember. On a wall chart we posted by each one's name the amount of time in which the listeners were able to summarize the other's comments.

These entry activities contained an assured success, drew on what students habitually do anyway—tell what they think and feel and remember what others say—and enlisted those processes for an academic purpose.

CLASSROOM ORDER

Order in the classroom was a challenge, so the second day we introduced a new way to obtain it.

"This morning I would like to do something different with you," I said. "We'll be starting and stopping a lot, so I need to agree with you on a signal to use to end what you're doing so that everyone stops at the same time. Otherwise it won't work. We would use too much time going back and forth. So what would be a good signal? Should I just say 'Stop' or would it work better to say 'Class'?"

They considered this in silence, so I continued.

"If I say 'Class!' loud enough would everyone stop?" I asked. Their silence signaled, I felt, their pending decision whether to cooperate with me and agree to anything that limited them. They regarded me warily.

"Or how about if I clap my hands? Is that better? What would be a good signal to get your attention?" My questions communicated my expectation that we would focus their attention. Asking them to help me select a signal conveyed three presumptions I wanted to leave unargued that (1) their activity would have a pattern, (2) everyone would participate, and (3) we would use an efficient signal. The nature of the signal was incidental but helping to choose it gave them a sense of ownership and an impression of an orderly activity to come.

"Say 'Shut up!'" one student finally said.

"How about a word like 'Philadelphia'?" another suggested.

"I'd like just to try saying 'Class,'" I said, "and then if something more is needed, I'll clap my hands. And if that doesn't work, we'll try something else. So what I'd like you to do is to go ahead and talk for a half-minute and we'll try it out, okay?" I looked up at the clock while they began talking. The volume soon increased.

"Class!" I said, and began counting seconds silently. Soon the noise abated. "That took seven seconds and everyone was quiet," I said. "Maybe we can just use that. That was great! Do you get the idea? We'll practice it some more. It's actually fun to stop in mid-sentence because then you know you've really got control of yourself and you can remember what you were saying. When I say 'Please continue,' you can go on right from the middle of the sentence where you left off. If you're in a small group, people will say 'You were the one talking' and you can continue from where you were. Let's try it again. Go on and talk for a while." The noise built again.

"Class!" I said, and counted seconds. "Three seconds! All right! Far out! Okay, now try it again."

"Did we break our record?" a student asked.

"You're setting a record every time now," I answered. "Go on and do it some more." They were so keyed to the process that they found it hard to talk, and instead began thumping chairs and desks.

"Class!" I said, and then a moment later, "One second! Yay!" They applauded for themselves. I then explained a new activity, began it, and soon wanted their attention.

"Class!" I said. Noise continued. I looked at the second hand of the clock and began counting aloud: "Seven seconds, eight seconds, nine seconds, ten seconds, eleven seconds . . . ." There was silence.

"Okay," I said, "that took eleven seconds, not too bad." Looks of pleasure appeared on some faces. In a real situation they had applied the rule agreed on.

Mr. Dawson then introduced a new rule. He would give them a brief cushion of time after saying "Class" in which they could finish their sentences and return to their seats if they were away from them. After five seconds he would begin counting. For all the time accumulated through the morning, the entire class would remain in silence past their time to leave for recess or lunch.

The same method worked to maintain attention as noise arose during an activity. Mr. Dawson would raise his hand to indicate that they were accumulating time. This usually motivated them to quiet each other whenever he said "Class!" Often they were totally quiet in one or two seconds.

DR. JENSEN'S MESS

In the next several days we began to ask them to explain to each other points of knowledge in their subjects, calling these Learning Feats. Soon students realized that they actually knew answers and could express them, and their sense of success and optimism about learning slowly grew.

Our random assignment of pairs for learning practice stressed some students by putting them with others they didn't like. One boy refused to cooperate with the girl sitting next to him. Guessing that even a tiny motive might alter his attitude, I caught up with him at the water fountain.

"Look," I said, "I'll give you fifty cents if you will pair up with her." He appeared startled, thought a moment, and nodded. I drew two quarters from my pocket for him. He returned to his seat and from then on cooperated.

One small boy interrupted constantly till one day I called him to where I was sitting, and drew him up onto my lap (not something one would do presently). He sat still and looked up at me, his feet swinging off the floor. I pretended that he was a first grader to whom I needed to give extremely explicit, patient directions, and from that point, he changed. Yet even with many small improvements, students often were inattentive, and Mr. Dawson in frustration would make critical remarks to the class.

When we discussed these situations, he realized that criticism was counterproductive and made an important shift. He approached students individually, eyeball to eyeball, said in a respectful tone of voice that he was disappointed in their behavior and told them what he wanted them to do. Behaviors changed further. Even so, several activities we tried were beyond their skills and would degenerate into disorder. Toward the end of the first week, a student came to Mr. Dawson.

"Are we going to have that Dr. Jensen mess again?" he asked indignantly.

TRUE FEELINGS

An incident occurred in the second week that changed them. From being artificial, guarded, and focused on external behavior, our activities became internal to them, occupying their emotions, shifting motivation from outer to inner.

One morning while I observed, Mr. Dawson asked each student in turn to give a single word that described his or her feeling right then. The fifth student he questioned was a boy slumped in his chair who answered in a low voice, "Sad."

When others had answered, Mr. Dawson began around a second time with "What was it that gave you that feeling?" This time, the boy choked out, "My aunt died last night."

There was confusion and silence. All were stunned. Many had known his aunt and were closely attuned to each other's moods but had no idea how to respond. Mr. Dawson expressed his own feelings of sadness, invited the boy to tell what had happened, and then asked others to share what they felt about what he had said.

Several offered comments of grief, sadness, and sympathy, and a couple were crying. With the emotions of the moment potent but unfinished, the next event was a watershed. Mr. Dawson asked if others would like to tell an experience of their own with death or loss. Nearly everyone's life had been touched with something painful, and in the next half-hour shared their stories while others listened closely.

A profound softening of atmosphere occurred. They realized that they were not as isolated as their prior hostility had made them appear. The death of the boy's aunt was a gift to the class, making it legitimate to talk frankly about heartfelt needs and feelings. They had let themselves be touched genuinely, and we needed to sustain that opening by helping them provide high quality attention to each other.

The incident suggested a strategy any teacher might hold in reserve for the right moment: Prepare to respond constructively to unexpected trauma or disaster by drawing out its impact and learning. Any school year may contain events that affect everyone and temporarily free positive emotions from their restraints. The teacher can respectfully open a way for each to express the meaning of an event for them, generating a new focus of awareness. Expressed with considerateness and relevance to the day's happenings, their new feelings are a powerful lever for accepting new learning about themselves and each other.

COMMUNICATION SKILLS

As I went in each day, we repeated familiar program elements and steadily added new ones. The Communication Skills Check Sheet (Appendix 9) was a staple to improve the quality of both their social contact and academic work. We divided them into discussion groups of three and four for eight minutes, asked them to check themselves on the CSCS, and then next time the student on their right. They cooperated readily, enjoyed rating themselves and each other, and became more receptive to working with different people. As they memorized the points on the CSCS, we plotted their progress visibly on a wall chart, and did the same with rules for remembering.

APPRECIATION TIME

Affecting the classroom atmosphere also was the Appreciation Time Mr. Dawson led daily. The activity began haltingly, but the class soon insisted on it. He would call on them individually by name, they would stand, and he would ask each one the same question: "Can you name someone who has given you a good feeling?" They would say a name and then sit down.

One day, several named five or six others; a couple, ten or twelve others, while everyone listened attentively. They had played a team sport during lunch period and had many sources of good feelings. Two said, "Everyone in the class is my friend."

When everyone had responded to the question, I assumed they were done, but Mr. Dawson started around again, asking "Could you describe one specific thing someone did to give you a good feeling?" They answered with wide grins and rapt attention, even students who two weeks before had been isolated and withdrawn. I had the impression of deep hungers satisfied in this forty-five-minute exercise.

From that point, playground disciplinary problems all but disappeared. The student who had complained about "Dr. Jensen's mess" came to the teacher again.

"Mr. Dawson," he said, "we don't think this is Dr. Jensen's mess anymore."

Some individual changes were by unobtrusive self-management. One boy who had not been able to restrain his tendency to interrupt undertook giving himself a grade every fifteen minutes for how well he had controlled himself that period, and gradually modified his behavior (cf. 17). A student rejected by others had previously retaliated with insults, yet as his own mood and actions improved, he found acceptance in the group.

At the end of the second week, Mr. Dawson asked the students to write a note to me about what, if anything, had changed for them as a result of our work together. Each noted an improvement, such as these five:

> Before you came our classroom was a disaster. Now we've become a little better. But we still need a little bit more improvement. Mr. Dawson has gotten better too. He doesn't have to raise his voice anymore. —Damiko

I have noticed a change in the classroom. Now they don't talk out that much. They know how to control themselves better than before. I know how to control myself and my temper. You have done a lot for this class. —Aaron

You have made me feel like I can learn about people I never knew about. And I thank you because the class is much better now. —Florence

When you came our class started to listen more. We are glad you are helping us with our problems. —Jolenta

We have changed. Even I have changed. If you didn't come to this class, we would never have changed. I like you very much. —Dominique

ORGANIZATION GROUPS

To enable them to take more responsibility for their learning, Mr. Dawson and I organized the room into groups of four to six students. We began by asking them to list privately the names of others they felt they "could best learn from" and those they "would like to be with in a group." Collating their responses, we identified those named least (who needed the most support), identified others they liked who could be a bridge into group acceptance, and assigned them together.

Multiple nominations identified those likely to be accepted as leaders. The five captains we selected met with the teacher for training and talked out an agenda to introduce to their groups. They might help their group select a group name, instruct their group in learning activities the teacher initiated, report on the progress of their individual members, reinforce good communication skills of their group, help those who had problems with schoolwork, and design some of their own activities. Some groups were immediately successful at working together while others needed help. Some responsibilities were shifted, but soon cooperative energy was flowing.

One day the Seattle Deputy Superintendent of Schools, Mona Bailey, came to visit. Mr. Dawson chose to demonstrate small group sharing along with self-rating on the CSCS. Ms. Bailey sat nearby and listened in on one of the groups. Afterward she spoke to its leader who was near me.

"What's changed for you in the last couple weeks?" she asked.

"I used to go home and beat up on my little brother all the time, but I don't do that anymore," the boy said cheerfully. He was now helping his group keep on task with an energy that appeared to be natural leadership ability.

I hadn't visited for several days when the teacher called to tell me that the students wanted to show off some of the Learning Feats they had mastered. At the appointed time, he drew names at random from a sack. Students came two at a time to the middle of the room where two chairs faced each other. They took the seats and in turn asked each other a question drawn randomly from math, language arts, and history. They answered confidently and returned to their desks, clearly delighted with their effort.

Mr. Dawson told me that the specific feedback they had obtained through measuring talking time on their learning tasks had created a sense of excitement, enabling them to compare how well each was doing. It was competitive, he noted, but not in a way that anyone felt put down. Rather, all seemed stimulated by it and worked harder. After we had worked together for a few weeks, the mood and activity in the classroom had changed significantly. Students welcomed me into the class with smiles and greetings, and one day a group leader approached me during a break.

"Are you going to write a book about this?" he inquired.

"Yes I am," I said and laughed.

"Will you put our names in it?" he asked with an excited smile.

"I'd be glad to," I said. They were Brett Fashaw, Alexis Mitchell, Dominique Michael, Tameka Green, Ikenna Joku, Adjovi Casselle, Michael Ellis, Mateen Abdullah, Darrel Holman, Kiasha Thomas, Fredrika Fisher, Maxie Jamal, Jolenta Coleman, Edward Roy, Curtis Riggins, Ardess Ballard, Ira Thomas, Dural Thomas, Kelton Dorsey, Damiko White, Aaron Johnson, Niyah Shields, Mandalin Richardson, Florence Paige, and Tavia Hinton.

BEGINNER'S MIND

"I had to adopt a beginner's mind about this," Mr. Dawson said to me. He had decided to be teachable, and understood that he needed to change his intentions, manner of interacting with students, classroom control, and design of learning. A new habit he felt was significant was catching each student privately every day to make a supportive or encouraging comment to them.

Yet changing the class had been easy. He had tried my suggestions, we solved problems together, and students followed his direction willingly. Activities were successful and pleasant, and by the end of the school year, six weeks after our start, the room had been transformed.

The cumulative impact of different ways to express natural motivations layered upon each other. The activities were not an extra spliced in occasionally but were the manner of accomplishing their central work. What they assimilated first period about giving attention to each other applied to their learning activity in second period. The third period's sharing of good feelings infected the mastery practice during fourth period, and so on.

Activities converged: understanding the subject, organizing it so it could be practiced, practicing it, scoring it, performing it to the class, improving communication skills, and addressing feelings. Students experienced a teacher's enthusiasm, establishing a verifiable goal of mastery, getting the answer under their control, the pleasure of talking about what they knew, being assessed as successful by a peer, having their achievement quantified precisely, becoming competent with explaining their knowledge, and having their scores posted for public recognition. Here were the main components of the Practice Makes Permanent approach.

Seven core elements characterize it. Five help to master knowledge, two create a positive atmosphere, and fifty-four activities apply them.

Understand: Students understand what is conveyed or presented.
Organize: They organize it to make it easy to practice, save, and retrieve.
Practice: They assimilate knowledge by explaining and expressing it.
Score: They score their learning objectively by counting points of knowledge gained or timing their explanation.
Perform: They stand and perform what they know.
Good feelings: They give each other good feelings.
Communications: They improve the quality of their communications.

The methods are not separated by grade level because first graders can become as proficient at many of them as older students. Fresh energy steadily comes available from understanding, organizing, talking, mental review, self-rating, feedback, performing, scoring, communicating, and sharing good feelings. The effort needed is commonplace, students' manner of learning not that different one to another, and the outcomes not hard to achieve. We direct students to accumulate and save knowledge hour by hour.

Chapter Two

Quick-Start Methods

The methods in this chapter applied together enable students K–12 to experience steady increments of success and validation. To adapt practice to the youngest, cf. 34. Primary Grades.

1. ORGANIZE NOTEBOOKS

Students' notebooks are the main tool organizing their effort. To make content easy to practice and absorb, we separate questions from answers like a test. Then even working alone they can read a question, recall what they can about it, and turn to answer pages to fill in details omitted. The steps help them arrange it for multiple subjects. If you see them only for one subject, separate questions and answers to different pages:

"Open your loose-leaf notebook." If they use a wire-bound notebook, see comment below.

"Make the first page of the notebook the table of contents." They write that title on the first page and fill in the page later as they organize their notebooks.

"Make a section for each subject in the order you have them through the day." Use section dividers or write the names of subjects at the top of separate pages. Title a section Miscellaneous for their learning from experiences, reading, and alternate sources.

"After each subject title, add a half-dozen blank pages." See that everyone has several sheets after each subject.

"Title the first page after each subject divider Questions and the second, Answers." On the latter page and those after it, students write a summary of everything they learn about the subject, including references to a text or other sources.

For interest, suggest an alternate title for their Questions page. "Learning Feats" hints at preparation for public performance. If they object to writing out a separate page for questions, ask them to title it "Exam Questions." Schedule a test for the next day, dictate questions they copy exactly, and to that list add later a question for everything you want them to know for the semester. Check that their numbers for questions and answers dovetail. Ask them to print their notes to make them more legible and shareable.

If they use a wire-bound notebook already divided into subject sections and cannot shift the pages, title the first page of a section Answers. Write answers in it starting from the front and proceeding toward the back as usual, generating a summary of all the knowledge you want learned in that course. Title the last page of the section Questions and number these pages from the back of the section toward the front. When the question and answer pages meet, start a new notebook or open a new section in that one.

2. UNDERSTAND

Notice how you use input and output to transmit understanding.

Input

In the physical setting, remove or calm distractions. If their minds are on earlier events, bring them into the present.

Focus their attention on what you are about to say, and ask for their eyes on you.

Speak with a clear voice enunciating all words.

Check hearing. Those in back rows may miss low-volume or quickly spoken words. Many may have hearing deficits from excessive use of earphones. Find out which do and seat them closer to you. Monitor what they grasp.

Stay with simple, specific words that form a mental picture.

Use gestures, visual aids, and diagrams as appropriate.

Proceed with explanations step by step, creating an impression their short-term memory can grasp.

Write out key points on the writing board to examine part by part. They ask questions as needed and shift their attention from one part to another as it stands before them on the board, in a book, in their notes, or in your words.

Forecast an occasion of its use: that it will be tested, explained to a partner, presented to the class, or written. They retain better what they code as autobiographical, as something about themselves: "I'm going to stand and explain this."

Point out a common aim to adopt with them: That you can obtain their attention quickly, communicate a direction just once, and have everyone get it. You might initiate a little self-rating box on the board: "What grade should we give ourselves today for getting directions on the first try? How many times did we have to repeat them?"

Output

By their output of knowledge, students form it into a model they can express. What they say assures you that they received what you sent.

Ask someone to explain back what you said, or ask a question and pause before drawing a student's name randomly so that everyone formulates an answer.

You may ask them to explain specific, individual points to another student for a minute to give small doses of practice putting words to ideas.[1]

Expecting a student to explain something after rudimentary exposure to it may seem optimistic, yet a gradient develops. With one bit of knowledge, they repeat it. With two, they can focus on one or the other and can compare, contrast, separate, and sequence. With three, they move to whole and part, relationships, and causal links. Possibilities increase with each new point added, inviting a synthesis of how everything goes together.

Make your questions open-ended: "Tell us about . . ." or "Would you explain (show) how . . .?"

Monitor changes in their energy, how they assimilate what you present, and possible distractions. Make your instruction and directions clear:

Put away your books. You're going to take a test.
Please take out a clean sheet of paper.
Copy this down exactly.
Please close your books and stand up. We're going to do something different.
Work with your partner to develop a summary of what is outlined on the board.
Pair up for the next hour and explain your summary to your partner. When your partner knows it, raise your hand.
Ask each other all the questions we have studied this week. Switch back and forth with each question. When you both know them all, let me check you.

In saying anything at all you press them to pay attention but may inadvertently leave them confused. Was your comment a passing one, a housekeeping issue? Was it a learning that appears unimportant because you leave it and go on? What are they to do? Imagine their energy coming to a stop whenever you speak. They wonder, "Do I go this way or that? What's coming next? How do I cope?"

Sorting through your words, they must separate out what to hold onto. To apply themselves to one point and not another, they must tell them apart. Meet this constant need for a clear focus by summarizing in writing the learning they will assimilate.

3. HARD COPY

Students depend on hard copy for much of their learning and fill in missing pieces by revisiting it. There are several ways to provide it:

You write it fully on the board for them to copy.
They copy it from reference sources.
They write complete notes under your oversight or dictation.
They have a book they can mark up and keep.
You give them a detailed handout.

Writing your own summary is preferable because: (1) You can integrate threads from varied sources. (2) It more easily parallels your spoken presentation. (3) You clarify the points you expect them to retain out of everything you present. (4) It paces your expectations. You would love to deliver a feast of knowledge *globatim* but must wait patiently while they chew morsels. Writing what matters most, you discipline your expansiveness and focus their effort. (5) Having a defined, orderly form for their work increases their desire to claim it. With a hole puncher, comb bindings, and cover stock, every year students can make a book out of all their concentrated learning.

The more mature the class, the less they need to depend on you for gathering, presenting and organizing their material (cf. 43. Divide Subjects).

4. LEARNING FEATS

Once their learning content is in visible form, they can practice it to make it their own.

Our culture typically quantifies feats to honor a competency and distinguish it from others as in the Olympics motto, *Fortius, altius, citius* (stronger, higher, faster). We apply such energy and precision to the mastery of learning. Casting it as a performance after special preparation, we draw on a familiar frame of reference.

A Learning Feat thus is a chunk of learning a student can explain without help, scored by points or time, and organized in hard copy. The student masters it by Partner Practice (cf. next section) or other means, explains it to another student, a parent, or the class; is awarded its precise score (cf. Chapter 7); claims it as part of his or her permanent learning (cf. 51. Academic Mastery Report); and can replicate it any time.

For the uninvolved, the content is less important at first than their realization that they learn. On my first day with a severely emotionally disturbed high school boy, I let him pick what he wanted to study. Unwilling to speak a word to me, he pulled a *Far Side* cartoon book from the shelf.

Twenty minutes later, to quantify his progress, I asked him to tell me the cartoons he could remember. Without hesitating, he described seventeen in sequence from memory, a remarkable accomplishment revealing a concentrated mind that was his start into classroom cooperation.

5. PARTNER PRACTICE

After students receive a chunk of knowledge and write it out as question and answer, they pair with a partner, hand each other their notebooks, and ask and answer the questions. An hour usually begins with reclaiming prior material. Invite them to start partner practice on their own:

> When you walk in, find your partner, sit down and begin your mastery review. Listeners, go over your partner's notebook and ask any previous questions to help him or her maintain the answers. Speakers, tell your partner which questions you need to practice, and fill in parts you're missing.

After a few minutes at that, go to the day's new material.

Partner Practice Steps

Have them copy the following and check themselves against the list until they carry out the steps seamlessly:

1. Identify your partner for the day.
2. Sit where you can hear each other while speaking softly.

3. Listen for the teacher's signals to begin and end the activity.
4. Choose who speaks first and then trade roles.
5. Pick the questions and communication skills you will practice.
6. Listener asks the speaker questions from the speaker's list.
7. Speaker practices answer till ready to score it.
8. Listener records score under the question along with his or her initials.
9. Listener turns in score to teacher for posting.

Before scoring "for the record," students may take a day or more to practice an answer. The score either counts the points of knowledge in an answer or times its explanation to the second. The listener records the speaker's score in the speaker's notebook under the question. When prior material is re-scored, a new, higher count is entered if the mastery level increases (or a lower count if it declines). By maintaining accurate scores for each question, at any time you can add up the last figure under every question back to the beginning of the term to obtain a reliable total of the student's current knowledge. Post this on the room's scoreboard (cf. Chapter 7).

The number of points awarded to a question is just the number of points of knowledge in the answer that you would credit if they appeared on a test, usually one sentence of new material per point. Many questions may elicit discrete pieces or steps you would mark wrong if missing. If there are six points in an answer and the speaker tells them all, the listener jots down a 6 with his or her initials beside it in the speaker's notebook. For examples of scoring, cf. sections 46 and 54.

Point out skills you want them to use as they help each other. From the lists below, add a new item daily. Eventually, convert each list to a Learning Feat they memorize so they have clearly in mind many ways to help each other.

Nine Ways to Help Your Partner Learn

1. Listen silently while your partner recalls everything he or she can.
2. Ask your partner to explain what he or she knows, from least to best.
3. Help improve or expand answers.
4. Summarize answers and write them out completely.
5. Correct errors.
6. Identify what's most important.
7. Offer images, analogies, and ways to remember.
8. Give a personal touch to the knowledge.
9. Combine small answers into larger ones.

As their confidence grows, speakers can invite listeners also to ask questions in a different form, draw out ideas behind the speaker's answers, and help them reorganize the knowledge.

Ten Partner Communication Skills

1. Look at the speaker.
2. Feel respect and consideration.
3. Ask questions.
4. Take an interest in what they say.
5. Remember what they say.
6. Use their words and ideas.
7. Note similarities and differences compared to your ideas.
8. Check out your guesses about their thoughts and feelings.
9. Give compliments.
10. Tell what helped you.

Assign new practice partners when you want to broaden connections and reinforce interest in prior material. Facing a new person is a new demonstration of competence. To the same person our presentation may seem unneeded. We already showed them that we know it. A new face invites recasting the material, employing social skills, and keeping the knowledge fresh.

Bracelet Aid for Pairing

If your class has stable numbers and you want to partner everyone systematically, list them all in a column with names evenly spaced apart. Crop the column into a long strip with no margins at the top or bottom. Form it into a loop, and tape the bottom and top together like a bracelet with the names around the outside.

To match names, crease the bracelet between two names, smooth it out from the crease, and hold the two sides flat together with a paperclip. Pairs of names are back to back. Turn the bracelet back and forth to read off the matches. The next day, remove the clip and advance the crease.

The bracelet gives different results with even and uneven numbers because for every jump of the crease one name moves down and another up, passing each other two names at a time. If an uneven number are in the class, the cycle takes in everyone eventually. Advance the crease between the next two names, clip the bracelet, read off the pairs, and repeat daily till all have been matched. One person at the opposite end from the crease is always unpaired. You can partner with that student yourself or make a triad.

Pairing an even-numbered class that way, however, half would never be paired with the other half. Accommodate by advancing the names on one side past the names on the other just one position at a time. One side of the bracelet in effect holds still while the other moves just to the next name opposite. On alternate days the crease would then occur in the middle of a name instead of between two names. Rather than creasing through a name, let the names float at both ends of the clipped bracelet and match those two together. On the next day the crease is again between two, the following day they float, and so on. Eventually everyone is paired with everyone else.

Gradual Entry

When students are passive, hesitant, or resistant, change their behavior unobtrusively. Engage them in an activity that contains the change you want, arrange for them to succeed at it, and acknowledge their success. They don't notice the change until after it has occurred. They flow with the activity of the moment and find themselves with a new skill.

Put them in the easiest role first from which they can observe others' successful activity. Taking a helping role as a questioner in Partner Practice, they learn the format and subject matter. Counting up and recording their partner's points or time, they learn the scoring method, and watching someone else "doing it right," they increase their confidence that they can also.

Most can imitate a partner readily when roles are reversed, but some may also need the day's lesson presented individually: A helper (1) identifies the material to be mastered, (2) checks the student's notebook for questions written separate from answers for easy practice (cf. section 1), (3) explains points one by one: "Here are the four points that answer the question . . . . ." (4) The student tells the points back immediately. (5) The helper notes a score under that question in the student's notebook, and (6) at the end of the session, sees that scores are added to the student's total on the classroom scoreboard the same as for others (cf. Chapter 7). If the student has not yet mobilized himself or herself to write the questions and answers, photocopying another's notes can accommodate him or her temporarily.

Remedial sessions can be clearly focused: "Learn these five questions and tell them back either to me or to your partner." Provide targets: "We'll cover twenty points today. Please have all the answers copied down, and explain them to your partner without looking at them." For increasing the efficiency of transitions between individual and partner work, cf. "Resolve structure" in 39. Use Maps.

6. MAINTAIN ANSWERS

Be alert to your responses to this section. It may challenge assumptions. Maintaining answers deliberately instead of allowing them to fade is a paradigm shift, dependent on a conscious decision to conserve knowledge from when it is first presented.

Doing so depends on taking regular time to recall it. This is so fundamental yet so contrary to common practice that it bears repeating: If your students are not saving knowledge and are not taking regular time to recall it, connect the dots. The most direct way to ensure that they save knowledge is to practice recalling it. There are many ways to do that—writing, rewriting, reorganizing, speaking to a partner, speaking to a group, testing, performing, structuring, and mentally reviewing. One way or another they must draw out and express what has gone in.[2]

After the practice linked to the initial presentation, a logical time to maintain answers is at the start of the same class the following day. They save the prior before adding more. Whenever they have a day's work well absorbed, they use the remaining time to deepen prior work. Occasionally they can take a full period to practice prior material and incorporate outside learning.

Without such an active intent, learning turns vague. Though the superficiality of much learning hour by hour must be obvious to everyone, schools almost universally implement the Learn and Lose System. Enveloping most classrooms is a pattern leaving nebulous learning along the entire scale of ability. Students expect to forget most of what they take in. Even many high on the grading curve are abysmally ignorant. Ten influences designed by adults and beyond students' control describe their experience:

1. Courses begin and end by plan. Students know they will not be called on for their knowledge after the course, encouraging them to do the minimum and remain on the surface.
2. No intent to learn a body of knowledge. Students are not asked to master a comprehensive explanation but rather to qualify—to pass, be eligible for sports, satisfy parents, or obtain further education. Temporary knowledge does this.
3. Adults mastering a subject maintain a hard copy. We buy the book or make detailed notes. In schools, textbooks are returned and notes thrown away. Without them, a student cannot update nor review tenuous learning, and fragmented ideas are not made whole.
4. Small pieces are not integrated. Exam questions are often atomized into terms, formulas, and parts not conceived as a system with structural harmony.

5. Tests supply the information needed and students only recognize a correct answer. They are not expected to supply structure and details.
6. Personal interest is usually irrelevant. Instead of expanding the curriculum, it is usually "no credit." Students' interests compete with education.
7. Reviews for the test constrict both the content and the time to focus on it. Near exam time, teachers provide a summary of the course from which they draw the test. By studying review questions, students pass respectably, rendering other class hours forgettable.
8. Multiple exams back to back in a few days encourage cramming. Data run through the mind may be unarticulated, disorganized, based on memory alone instead of understood, and installed under pressure—and lost as rapidly as it was gained. A master teacher described giving the previous semester's final exam to the same students a month later without notice. All scores declined drastically and many A grades reverted to F.
9. Courses typically have a final exam marking the last time the school calls on the student to know the subject. Knowledge is released to evaporate.
10. Learning and nonlearning are accepted equally. Students with a D grade may receive no followup to bring it to a B, so that those at the low end continue to drop out. They need a return loop back to effort that assures results.

Learn and Save

Education's purpose is learning retained, that knowledge should persist in students' minds. The Practice Makes Permanent design offers a means: learn, record, and save. Make a hard copy, divide it into questions and answers, practice answering the questions, and maintain them.

To do this while changing nothing else in your teaching methods, draw all tests from everything you have taught them. The longer students are with you, the more depth and mastery they should have of everything you have worked on together because you test it cumulatively.

Every exam can also summarize everything important treated to that point: "You're responsible for a 100% score on this test maintained to the end of the term." After the first test, go over all the questions anyone missed and repeat it. They continue to retake the test until they obtain a perfect score and then do so again or until you sign them off as having mastered it. Looking forward to this would urge everyone to study for permanence from the start.

Another way is to revisit course material instead of prior tests. Material from your earliest lessons with them would be fair game for current tests. Half of any test might cover current material and half draw from prior.

In both elementary and high schools, teachers can team up to take advantage of a longer time frame and hold students responsible for sustaining their learning for two years. One teacher might confirm work begun by several others with either of the designs above. Making all the previous year's material available for inclusion in current tests would largely offset the impact of the Learn and Lose System.

The scoring method described here helps students maintain learning by making clear where practice is needed. They can increase scores on prior tests and raise any course grade from the past two years by retaking tests and demonstrating further mastery.

Ordinary experience affirms the value of sustained attention to memory. A retired systems analyst tells me that she still retains the squares of all numbers up to twenty-five that she learned in high school. Perhaps you have opened a box of school memorabilia and noted reports, assignments, and collections of information but before you open them, the material is unavailable to your conscious mind. Had you wished to render it usable throughout your life, leafing through it the first week of each January would have been sufficient. Because you did not draw on it and made no effort to recall it, all of it disappeared from your mental toolkit. Few people retain knowledge without deliberate effort to recall or use it.

Pondering this, a teacher might slap himself upside the head and exclaim, "Of course! The reason students don't remember anything is that we don't ask them to remember anything. Of course!" Only deliberate effort saves vague learning.

7. IMPROMPTU PERFORMANCE

Performance here means explaining a chunk of learning before others. Teachers draw on students' needs for attention, acceptance, and approval by asking questions of them, but a performance is more significant. A public challenge stimulates students to raise their competence. They want to demonstrate what they master, and not what they know vaguely. They want to claim a personal achievement: "I'm confident of this and now I'm going to show you."

For those who would rather have a sharp stick in the eye than stand and perform, we calm their fear in steps. They explain their knowledge to others one to one until they have mastered it, so that their performance to class or parents is an assured success.

Announce an Impromptu Performance whenever you have a spare three to five minutes. You can (1) ask them to tell back their entire current day's mastered learning, or ask a question (2) from their notebooks, (3) from a bag of slips with questions they have learned that day, (4) from a cumulative bag holding all past questions, or (5) from their personal expertise (cf. section 42).

Read the question aloud, look at everyone, and pause briefly, hinting "This could be yours. Are you up to it?" While you count to ten, they draw on their mental stores and call up their knowledge.

Draw a name randomly from a bag of class names to avoid unconscious patterns. Eager students overshadow others and teacher predilections may give unhelpful messages.[3] Because it is distasteful to embarrass anyone, I prefer not to call on students who I believe do not know the answer or who have an off-putting personality. Chance selection distributes attention fairly, and drawing from all names helps prevent anyone from slacking off.

To provide everyone equal turns at standing and performing, you can set aside their names once they perform until the whole class has done so, and then start over. This leaves a growing number coasting, however, knowing they will not be called on. To keep them engaged, on random days draw a name from the cup of those who have already spoken, so that all have a motive to remain alert. The student selected stands up, states the question, performs the answer, takes questions from other students if asked, and sits down. Thank them and lead the class in applause. Hear from as many as time allows.

For added interest, you can reward everyone with Bonus Time if the questioned student performs competently, encouraging them to support each other's efforts (cf. 28. Use Consequences). Impromptu Performance at the end of a day (especially with a few minutes of Mental Movie, next) sends them out the door with their competence affirmed.

8. MENTAL MOVIE

Mental Movie deepens their knowledge and enables them to enjoy thinking about it. Use it whenever you have two to four minutes.

Ask them to sit upright, close their eyes, and calm their breathing. Focusing on the regular inflow and outflow of air helps their mind enter the alpha state that aids reflective thought. When they find their inner world steady, ask them to "run the movie" of everything they said, did, heard, read, wrote, practiced, performed, and learned from the start of the day as though they were viewing raw footage of a movie about themselves. If they have written a Peg List, they have already placed key ideas in sequence (cf. 31).

Ask them to confirm everything they learned that day and then work backward a day at a time, giving attention to four zones: (1) visual—images of pictures, diagrams, visible steps, use of board space, and borders around key ideas; (2) sounds of voices; (3) feelings and sensations; and (4) physical actions. Looking forward to this reminds them all day to notice details and write the script of their movie.

9. APPRECIATION TIME

Researchers studying aggressive and cooperative behavior among kindergartners many years ago noticed a pattern. They first counted a median of forty-two aggressive acts on the play field daily. Then they introduced a ten-minute sharing time when students could tell how others were friendly toward them during play that day, naming another student. There were soon "more buddies than bullies," and the median aggressive acts dropped to nine daily. When they changed the question to ask who was unfriendly toward them, the aggressive acts climbed back to forty per day. Returning to naming friendly actions, aggressive acts dropped again, this time to six.[4]

An exchange only slightly less direct has the same effect on adults. Typically when one in a group refers respectfully to another's idea, the second is given a green light to talk again. We feel more secure and accepted, and more ready to repeat what already brought approval. Appreciation Time fills a fundamental need in one with a genuine sentiment from another.

Give your students time each day to tell how others were friendly, helpful, or kind toward them, or gave them a good feeling.[5] Address each individually: "Who gave you a good feeling today?" and "How did they do that?" You can also use an Appreciation Board, a small bulletin board where they can write their positive thoughts about each other; thanks, admiration, gratitude, appreciation, help given, and skills they see others use.

Any class that "doesn't want to talk about those things" especially needs to. The harder it is for them to intend others' good feelings and express gratitude, the more they need it. The class described in Chapter 1 was at first fractured and hostile but in six weeks changed completely.

If they do not respond when you invite them to express appreciation, consider their silence a cry of desperation. Think about it: They are not aware of receiving good feelings from anyone. An alternate meaning is just as appalling: If they do express a good feeling, they fear the treatment they may receive. What an emotional desert, what a depressing situation in which to be forced to spend six hours a day. If some try to sabotage what you attempt, read the deeper message about their fear of self-exposure and their need for emotional safety, and keep at it.

They may find it safer to begin with sources of good feelings distant from the classroom. Refer them to an EXPERIENCE. They have tasted a dessert, taken a warm shower, fallen asleep comfortably, taken a hike on a sunny day. Draw out how their own activity generates feelings.

Then ask, "What THINGS give you a good feeling?" List objects like a bed, food, vehicle, sports equipment, musical instruments, videos, CDs, computer, cell phone, clothes, and so on. Let them fish around for how the use or possession of an object affects them. For those who play a ball game of some kind, a ball in hand changes their state instantly. How would they describe that?

Move toward animate objects: "How about ANIMALS?" How do they describe the feeling they get from petting their cat or playing with their dog?

"Now how about PEOPLE NOT PRESENT?" Can they think someone's action toward them recently that gave them a good feeling? When they identify a supportive person, ask them to describe the inward shift that occurs in them around this person. What generates a change? Some will note surface reciprocity during games, but draw out subtle details also like others' smiles, the sounds of their voices, phrases they use, or attitudes they manifest.

"Now how about anyone PRESENT?" Gradual steps stock their minds for noticing the personal and present. Spend as much time as they can use appreciating those in the room. These comments meet deep-seated needs, remedy hurts, displace feelings of devaluation, and are probably the most powerful force available for changing the atmosphere in your class.

You can personalize the topics in the appendices: "Tell about one of your best experiences with friendship," or "Tell about a time you helped someone who was down." Invite out the specifics of their experiences.

Saboteurs may talk about drug/alcohol or violent/destructive experiences, challenging you toward actions that could subvert your relationship with the group. They may hope to test your credibility about good feelings by jarring you into bad ones. Inquire whether their collective direction will be positive.

"Hmm, William. I'm not sure how to respond to that, given what we're talking about. Let me ask everyone: Do you think you are ready to talk about good feelings and how people give them to each other constructively?"

Cues aimed at the distracters are your answer. Allow others to show you. You might say, "Well, let's try it for a while. If you're not ready for it today, we can go on to the next section in math." Resume your hardest subject after these sessions if you can.

Other points can help them understand appreciation:

Positive leads to positive, negative to negative. Talk out how they carried an attitude from one setting to another, such as school to home or vice versa; or how one person's impact on them affected their relationship with someone else. What developed the tone originally, how was it transferred, and what was the result?

Everyone receives something. Have them count up how much has been provided for them: room, light, heat, paper, pencil, clothing, food, shelter, and so on. Who else had to labor, and where were they in the world for your students to have what they need? Make lists of what they receive and what they give back to the world, and compare them.[6]

Gratitude is the appropriate response for receiving. Let them discuss what they do when they receive from others. Who serves them, and do they respond well or poorly? Gratitude keeps them from viewing themselves as victims. Model it yourself.

Everyone can give something. Ask them to brainstorm what they could give back to the world and to others. Synthesize their discussion into a thoughtful question and answer they record in the Miscellaneous section of their notebooks.

How you respond to students personally is likely to arise from an individual style. You may feel naturally involved and readily interact with them, modeling skills easily or have a natural stance outside the group while tending to its needs. If you are among the latter, a middle ground is at least to allow them to practice relationship skills with you safely. If they try to involve you, play along.

Chapter Three

Communicate and Connect

With the basic success structure in place, we can attend better to the relationships students develop. The means discussed here bring rapid results. Students discover that they can connect directly by how they give attention and speak positively.

10. PERFECT CONVERSATION

On a Monday morning as I stood before my class of students aged twelve to fourteen, fresh in my mind was a gathering I had attended the night before. A roomful of adults had listened to and built on each other's ideas.

"I was in a perfect conversation last night!" I exclaimed. As I described it I realized that the skills could be taught, each one meeting a basic need. I wrote them on the board for everyone to copy.

1. Look at the speaker > attention
2. Leave a brief silence after each one speaks > respect
3. Include everyone > inclusion
4. Ask questions > be proactive
5. Connect with others' ideas > idea development

My students learned the five points as a Learning Feat, "What are the rules for Perfect Conversation?" Later we made up small groups in which they could practice them. I spurred their motivation by requiring that they complete five minutes using the skills perfectly before they could break for lunch, which they were able to do easily.

To try it, give everyone a handout or put the rules on the board (two skills added later were to accept feelings and use short messages instead of long speeches). Explain and discuss each and invite them to tell their experience with it, the need it meets, and the effects when it is ignored.

Divide the class into groups of four to six students. Ask each group to make a circle so they can see others' faces easily and no one is structurally excluded. Give them a time of three to five minutes and say, "See if you can do it." They will look at each other, scan the guidelines, someone will ask a question, and they are under way. As they are able to use the time, increase it. To monitor them, place your chair in the center of the room where you can hear them all.

A reinforcement such as Bonus Time may stimulate them to do the activity perfectly (cf. 28. Use Consequences). If you dismiss them to lunch or recess and can be flexible with your schedule, you might say:

> We have twelve minutes before lunch. Choose a timer for your group. When you think your group has done five minutes following all five PC rules perfectly, give me a signal. If I agree, you can leave early. Focus just on your own group and ignore others if they leave.

11. COMMUNICATION SKILLS CHECK SHEET

Students work best on communications when fresh from interactive activities. If time is available soon after lunch, you might alternate between using it for communications practice and an activity about feelings.

Students' skills can change quickly if you (1) explain a skill easy to apply, (2) provide them an experience in which they can practice it, (3) give them explicit recognition for doing so, and (4) add more skills. Either academic or experiential approaches work, but one may suit you and your students better. Use of a variety of means develops flexibility with the skills. Make a photocopy of the CSCS (cf. Appendix 9) for their notebooks.

Academic Approach

With students already somewhat disciplined, you can treat the skills like anything else to learn. Divide the check sheet into five Learning Feats, one for each major section with four to seven points in the answer. Discuss one skill a day, but also suggest that they pick one to apply deliberately: "Really put it to work. Plant it in your mind and think how to use it."

Younger students can practice the same skill taught to everyone, but those older may find this artificial and prefer an individual selection each practices unobtrusively.

Experiential Approach

You can also arrange experiences that elicit the skills, especially small group discussion. See **Use the Check Sheet** for options. Involving students may increase flexibility but also require more time. You might teach some skills academically and expand practice time as students use it well. Pause to let them check themselves on the CSCS after any interactive classroom work, and point out skills they use.

Check Sheet Content

Students of all ages need the skills, but the level of your class dictates where to start. A single skill such as "Wait until another finishes" can be important even for prekindergarten children. Several apply to the core issue of paying attention to another. Some refer to inner activities students are not accustomed to managing, but learning the inner along with the outer makes both easier. As needed, discuss each skill with your class:

1. What inner activities do you check before communicating?

    - Notice others' desire to speak. How can you notice that? How do you yourself show you are ready to speak?
    - Feel respect and consideration. How do these two qualities compare and contrast? What do you do inwardly to feel them?
    - Focus on the one speaking. How do you show that you focus?
    - Wait until the other finishes. How does it feel to wait while another searches for words?

2. How do you listen?

    - Look at the speaker. How does it feel when others look elsewhere while you talk? How can you tell if someone is ignoring you?
    - Don't interrupt. Say "Excuse me" if you do. How do they like being interrupted? What is their experience of having others say "Excuse me"?
    - Ask speaker to continue. How would they do this?
    - Leave a brief silence after a speaker finishes. Allowing silence after another talks makes it less likely for one person to dominate the group. The brief silence allows everyone to think about what was said, choose a better response, include everyone, and feel more respected.

3. How do you include everyone?

- Invite those to talk who haven't. How do you invite people? What would someone say to invite your thoughts? What feelings does it generate?
- Give equal time talking. How can you do this yourself or help others do it? How does it feel to hold back so someone else can talk?
- Ask questions and accept answers. What are their experiences, positive or negative, with others asking them questions? Discuss how they can accept answers without agreeing with them.
- Use others' names. Ask about their feelings of inclusion when they hear their name used.

4. How do you give a good feeling?

- Be interested in what others say. Hear their experiences of giving and receiving interest.
- Ask about their feelings and accept them. Discuss how they want their feelings treated. Do they think others are different?
- Thank people. How do they express gratitude? Do they like to be thanked?
- Give compliments. Explore compliments they could give; how appreciation, admiration, and respect differ, and what makes a compliment welcome or unwelcome.
- Tell what helped you. One of the best ways to give people good feelings is to let them know a positive impact they had: "You got my book for me. Thanks." "I could do it the way you explained it."

5. How can you connect to what others say?

- Remember what others say. Practice this fundamental skill in pairs, growing to longer remembering (cf. 12. Listen). You want them to decide consciously to remember what is said and done around them, a skill easily mastered.
- Use others' words and ideas. When they state an idea and someone else refers to it respectfully, how do they feel?
- Note similarities to and differences from your ideas. Discuss how people's ideas can be partly the same and different, and how they can accept both.
- Describe what affects you. The least intrusive way to enable another to change a negative behavior is to call attention to it neutrally. A kindergarten student froze when his teacher said to him seriously, "Do you realize you're hitting her?" Neutral information can change behavior when blame or criticism might generate tension:

"The noise makes it hard for me to concentrate." "After I spoke, you changed the subject so I thought you dismissed the point I was making." You describe behavior that had an impact on you.
- Check out your guesses about others' thoughts and feelings. Describe their behavior accurately and your guess about its meaning, but don't argue about what you think they feel. They are the authority: "Are you feeling sad? I noticed you frowning." "Did something special happen to you today? You seem really happy."
- Summarize others' thoughts and feelings. Attempt to describe and summarize accurately instead of judging. Practice lead-in phrases like "So you're saying . . . ," "You're feeling . . . about . . . ," "It's important to you that . . . ," "You want . . . ," and "You mean . . . ." Your intent is to express others' meaning accurately, not to instruct them in what they should say. Let the speaker correct the message: "No, I meant that . . . ."
- Talk out problems. They can describe situations they were in and tell what worked or not to resolve problems (cf. 16. Conflict Resolution).

Soon after introducing this set to a class, I arranged a discussion and asked them to select one skill to use. A student who often distracted the class with crude humor but was unusually attentive caught my attention. During the debrief, I asked him which skill he had chosen. "I was feeling respect and consideration," he said solemnly. His focus on a single quality changed his group's experience.

They realized for the first time that carrying out these steps required effort—to look for cues of others' desire to speak, to open inwardly to a feeling of respect, and to endure waiting. It startled them to admit that their discomfort at waiting drove them to interrupt.

These few guidelines make communication possible. Just looking at the speaker and not interrupting improve primary level communication vastly—two points worth discussing with them. What does it mean not to interrupt, and what is their experience with this? Because students often follow these rules spontaneously, you can readily affirm their successful practice from the start.

One first grade teacher divided her class into pairs, gave a topic, and asked the speakers to talk for a minute about it. Listeners did points 2a and 2b above, told back two things they remembered, and then traded roles. Within a few minutes, they had done three rounds with new pairs and topics. All seemed fascinated, delighted to be successful, and connect with others.

The following day a special teacher led the class and later asked the regular teacher, "What have you been doing with these children? They're more attentive, they're listening better and cooperating!" A few minutes of practice on one day had caused the class to change noticeably.

Fifth graders in one group had difficulty getting along with others. Just their willingness to be together and share a few comments constituted success. One day, however, an aggressive girl understood "including others." A boy absent for a couple sessions had returned but was paying no attention. The girl glanced at him off in his own thoughts, said his name, and asked, "What do you think about this?" His eyes changed as though jerked suddenly awake. He answered her question and began to participate. Even a single change can be significant for some students. Small steps done well eventually draw in all.

The intent to give others good feelings is glue binding a group together. We provide means to express this and recognition for doing so. Everyone wants to receive good feelings from others, but many do not know how to give them. At a dance once in early high school, I stood near an upperclassman who began punching me on the arm. Feeling assaulted, I was astonished later to hear his older brother say he liked me. Some students are slow to decipher the peer group relationship code. We need to teach them how to exchange good feelings.

Use the Check Sheet

1. Refer to the check sheet. During any small group activity, ask students to place the CSCS on their desks in front of them and refer to it periodically.
2. Observe. Ask them to watch others' actions and group incidents for the effect of skills used and how other skills could have influenced outcomes.
3. Select skills. Ask them to select skills to use for a day or in an upcoming activity and assess their experience later with a short debrief: "Which one did you choose? How did it work?" Telling them ahead that you will ask them to comment later spurs them to apply what they know.
4. Rank skills. Rank a skill set in order of their importance.
5. Add skills. Ask them to add one new skill per day to their repertoire. Invite them to share their experience of using it.
6. Rate themselves. Ask them to rate themselves after activities. After small group discussions on Monday afternoons, for instance, they turn to the CSCS in their notebooks and rate their use of each skill or those in a portion you designate. With elementary grades, a 0 to 3 scale is sufficient, where 3 = excellent use of the skill, 2 = moderate use, 1 =

some use, and 0 = not used at all. Upper grades can distinguish 0 to 10 levels of skill. Ask students to leave blank any skill that for some reason did not apply. A student might rate herself a 10 for "Looked at speaker," because she steadily paid attention to and looked at whoever was talking.

7. Rate others. When you have a series of small group discussions with stable groups, shift the manner of their rating from day to day. First they put their name at the top of the sheet and rate themselves. The next day, they hand their sheet (or notebook if they have inserted it there) to their left, rate the person whose name is on the sheet given to them, and then hand it back. On the third day, they hand it to their right, again rating the person whose name is at the top. On the fourth day they hand it across the group. Student comparing their self-rating with others' scores for them increases objectivity.
8. Use a skill overnight. They apply a skill at home overnight, and the next day they discuss the results of their effort.
9. Write feedback. On a poster, they write others' names and skills they saw used.
10. Practice reciprocity. To discuss understanding others accurately, refer to a game they know such as football or basketball that includes throwing and catching. Explain it as an analogy for communication. Invite their experiences of "when the ball was dropped" and why:
11. Skill tally. Pick out eight to ten communication skills important enough that you want students to receive daily feedback on them. To involve them in the selection, invite them to rate each skill on the sheet 0–10 for how important it is to them. Make a scoreboard (cf. Appendix 6) with the same number of columns and write a skill at the head of each column with student names down the side. When you see a student using a skill, without interrupting the lesson make a tally mark in the square beside the student's name and under the skill. Allow students to make tallies for each other, or select a couple at random who do tallies for that period.
12. Debrief. When you assign a communications task to students, always include a debrief afterward, even just for a minute. They describe what happened, rate their skill, or hear another's perception of their effort. When you set up an activity, the debrief helps complete the learning loop.
13. Students choose. For students edgy about cooperating, engage them in creating their own checklist. You can invite them to brainstorm how they want others to act toward them, and vote for their top ten suggestions. If they complain about others, they are making a point about how they want things to be, so extract that element: "So that's what you don't want. What does it imply that you do want?"

Many students at first misunderstand how to fill in the boxes of the check sheet, and mark all the columns across the entire page, making them unusable later. As you present it, draw a rough example of the sheet on the board and fill it in as you present it. Point out what a column is and the designated one for that day—furthest to the left with no marks in it yet. Explain the rating scale they are to use (e.g., 0 to 3), and offer examples of the rating levels.

Many students even in high school show their hunger for approval by giving themselves the maximum score immediately for each skill. They need massive, positive feedback before they can view themselves objectively. Just continue providing new occasions for ratings, and allude to a realistic perspective: "It's fun to rate your own actions, isn't it? Sometimes you can learn a lot." Using a scale of ten, at the start you can also ask them to rate themselves at a five, presuming a median ability until they understand it better, and giving them room both to improve or get worse.

Throwing and catching must be equal. If someone throws, someone else needs to catch or the ball is lost. You catch and throw an equal number of times and you throw to where the catcher is, not out of bounds where they can't get it. So adjust your words to what the other is ready to receive. And when you are the receiver, try to catch the meaning the other wants to send.

Turn around semantically negative statements into their implied positive. "I hate it when people interrupt me" becomes "I like people to let me finish my thought." "Letting people finish" then goes on their list to practice.[7] By identifying skills to post, they have already focused on each one, assessed its importance, and subconsciously bought into the idea of practicing it. Let them observe their peer and family interactions for several days to identify skills they might include. Discuss their findings, combine the similar, make a checklist, duplicate it or mount it on a poster, and tally their practice with it.

12. LISTEN

Communicating is easy to teach with a clear map, practice, and recognition. We start with a simple design and build more refined perceptions into it. With a few minutes a day at the next exercises, students learn to connect with others by speaking and listening. If you think negative attitudes could interfere, you might first employ Appreciation Time for several days (cf. 9).

The beginning is basic recall. Students hold in mind part of what they hear. Tell them "We're going to practice listening and remembering what others say. If you can do that, you can learn from everyone else's good ideas." Instruct them not to comment on what they hear. One teacher told first grade listeners, "Zipper your mouth so you won't interrupt," and they did so with dramatic gestures.

Select topics most can speak to, the more tangible for the younger: food, movies, games, pets, yards, their room, common experiences, and categories of favorite things. Appendices 2–5 have suggestions for different ages.

For many, having any answer is more important than an original answer. A parallel is the experience of a trainer who conducted many small groups in a leadership course. He reported that at first he wanted his adult male participants to supply their own answers to his questions. In time he found it more effective to have a prepared phrase for them to express in their own words. Training was less about originality than about focus, guiding them to notice a way of thinking.

If some appear unable to speak spontaneously about a topic, you can develop an overall answer with the class from which they can draw their own: "Here's what we've gathered. When you talk in pairs, mention the part that appeals to you personally." As they feel safe and successful, individualized answers emerge.

Use your assigned daily partners for this exercise if you have them (cf. 5), but for the extremely shy or self-conscious, even talking in pairs may be too demanding. Ask one to sit near a couple who "know how to do it" and watch "until you get the idea." Expect them to resolve their hesitance quickly. After others model for them once or twice, shift them to a pair. Offer a simple rule to determine who talks first, such as the one whose first name is first in the alphabet.

To start off, little time is needed for each turn; for first graders a minute or two and older students more. Increase the time as they accept each other, cooperate with new partners, and give each other good attention. After speakers' time ends, listeners recall what they heard. The little they retain from each others' words is significant as the first clue of their ability to absorb others' thoughts.

Content Varies

Primary students tell back one thing they can remember from what the speaker shared. Upper elementary, talking for a longer time, might select two or three points. Older students might try to summarize everything. With short time spans, everyone succeeds and increases their confidence in their listening.

When recall is done, recognition confirms the success of the listener. Ask students to raise their hands if their listening partner could recall what you asked. The reason for doing this is that student speakers typically do not think of the other person as the main actor. Their concern is themselves. By placing attention on their partner's accomplishment, they stretch their world, learn an essential element of listening, and become a source of recognition for each other.

If two behaviors make an activity work and the loss of either causes it to fail, then sensibly we encourage the weaker. Between speaking and listening, the latter is the problem. Most of its effort is internal and invisible in selecting, impressing within, and then recalling another's ideas. Speaking, on the other hand, they do automatically. To improve their thinking, most children need better listening that assimilates others' thoughts. For their partner experience, we don't want just speaking, but rather speaking to good listeners. If listening is good, the speaker's success is assured.

Many younger elementary students enjoy keeping score of the one thing they recalled in listening. Make a wall chart listing their names and a space beside each for a series of tallies, one for each point they remembered from their speaker. If you prefer not to have individual scores, use an all-class score. Tape a six inch wide strip of paper from floor to ceiling with two lines on it an inch apart up the center of it, forming an empty column. For every point anyone recalls from their partner's sharing, darken the column from the floor upward for an eighth of an inch. Recall of one point each by twenty students generates a two and a half-inch rise in the bar.

Their listening contains a life lesson. Ask them, "Why do we remember what others say? What happens when we don't?" Invite their stories about ignoring others' words or forgetting what they agreed to.

13. TOTAL ATTENTION

Listening begins with recalling what others say. Next we add the more subtle quality of caring. Students are often uncertain how to express supportive feelings and fail to realize the power of simple attentive presence.

Prepare for total attention pairs by having students learn and tell back the first set of skills on the CSCS, "What inner activity do you check before communicating?" Discuss how they notice others' desire to speak, give respect and consideration, and wait. The third section of the CSCS, "How do you give a good feeling?" is also helpful.

Explain the goal of giving attention and why it can be hard to do. It asks us to give up our own ideas. Someone else says, "I went to the beach," our thoughts go to our own beach experiences, and we want to tell about them. Our effort lies in halting our mind from flitting off to our own memories.

Developing in mind only what the other says amounts to a continuous sacrifice, giving a gift of providing a good speaking experience for the other. Their turn will come. Till then they release concern about their own thoughts and open instead to the picture the other paints.

Paying attention to the other, we represent inside us what this person is on the outside. We look at them, notice them but without making any judgment of them. We accept them as they are, and feel respect and consideration if we can.

It may help to demonstrate: Bring students into a tight circle around you so they can observe microbehaviors, and sit facing a student who will talk to you. Adopt an attitude of nonjudgmental acceptance, experience respect for the student, and become fascinated at their world. Then ask the class what they observed, and perhaps write what they saw as a checklist for their use.

Total Attention with Silence

Once they understand total attention, they try it out, doing their best to offer it as total, nonjudgmental, and nonintrusive. It generates safety and well-being in which peaceful reflection can emerge. It permits the speaker to be silent and for the inner consciousness to *be* before it must *do*; to rest in a steady flow of support before it must expend energy toward developing ideas.

Some students may feel anxious with silence at first because our culture trains us into constant activity. Provide alternate imagery:

> As you take your turn with your partner, think of laying on the side of a grassy hill on a warm day looking at the different shapes of the clouds. You and the person stop for a rest after an activity. There is nothing you have to do. You are simply with this person, paying attention to each other. We're in a classroom instead of on a grassy hill, but we can pay attention just as if we were outside in the sun. Please pair up, sit close by and face each other, and decide who is the first receiver of attention and the first giver of attention. (Wait till that is done). Now I ask the giver of attention to pay attention to the other in a general, overall way without expecting nor judging anything. Your job is just to absorb and appreciate this person. Receivers of attention, for this first round, I'll ask you not to say anything out loud. You only think while the other pays attention to you. Watch your thoughts come and go and allow the other person to give attention to you. There is nothing you need to do to earn the attention, nothing you need to say. Be who you are and allow the other to notice you. Relax and enjoy it. Please do this for one minute. Any questions? Ready? The minute starts NOW.

After a minute, debrief the experience. It generates subtly different ways of looking at their inner world. Start with those receiving the attention:

> In a minute, we'll reverse roles, so you'll get to play the other part. But for this round let's talk first with those receiving the attention. Receivers, how did you react inside? Was it hard or easy to relax? Was it hard or easy to accept the other's attention? Was it hard not to talk? Can you name the feeling it gave you? Can you identify any way your partner helped you even though he or she was not talking? Now to the givers. Givers of attention, what was hard and what was easy? Was it hard not to talk? Not to expect anything or make judgments? What did you notice about the receiver? Now would you both share with each other any positive thoughts that went through your mind, or any way you found a benefit from the exercise.

Have them reverse roles in the same pairs, repeat the same activity, and again debrief their experience in the new role. As they use the time well and realize that they are practicing a new skill, add more time to the exercise on later occasions. The few minutes needed to conduct it suggests that it can be readily spliced into a school day.

Total Attention with Talking

Previously, listeners learned to be quietly present to the speaker's world. They learned to withhold talking about their own ideas and restrain the urge to say, "I did that too!" Once they are successful at this, we want to stretch the same attitude and attention to include what their partner says. Dismissing their own thoughts, listeners aim just to absorb fully the picture the speaker develops and allow their imagination to be taken by the hand wherever the speaker wishes to lead. If they prefer to choose a topic first (cf. 14), point out that it need not limit them but can be a jump-off for exploring whatever comes to mind. You might begin with five minutes for speakers to talk and then increase the time gradually. Remind them that one student speaks at a time, give them a time limit, and begin:

> You can bring out a thought, talk about it, think a while, bring out another thought, look at the clouds, say something else. The other listens without interrupting, letting you explore whatever comes to your mind. You can think and talk with no pressure at all.

This sort of caring, undistracted attention has a powerful effect. As students probe their thoughts, others' acceptant attention sustains them in a way that it does not when they feel hurried or judged or obliged to comment immediately. Speakers learn to assemble their own thoughts without depending on others. They become better able to weigh their own ideas and experiences, shift perspective, and notice the impact of feelings. The essential condition enabling them to do this is knowing they will not be criticized nor analyzed but rather accepted as they are.

When speakers finish, listeners respond first with compliments, appreciation, or admiration and how they were personally helped by anything they heard. The speaker, in return, reinforces the listener's attention by telling what helped the speaker most (ignoring anything unhelpful). They notice how the quality of others' listening made it easier to develop their ideas.

After they have experienced this, you may want to deepen their understanding of it by discussing conditions that enhance it:

Respect and consideration
Privacy, not telling others what their partner said
Giving good feelings
Not applying labels
Developing their own ideas, images, and experiences
Not pushing their own thoughts into others' thoughts
When and how they have thoughtful silences with friends
Looking for the positive instead of the negative
Noticing what they can learn from others
Fascination at how others arrange their inner world
Assessing carefully what they want to talk about to a partner

With younger classes you might presume that they keep confidences and not even raise the possibility of breaches of trust. From mid-elementary onward some may have had their confidences misused and welcome discussion about how it feels to have others talk about them, and how they treat others' personal information. You might say, "In our discussions, there is no reason to talk about anything that puts someone down or could embarrass anyone else or yourself."

14. SELECT AND EXPLORE TOPICS

Selecting topics for group or class discussion enables students to think about what concerns them. The more committed they are to a topic, the better they cooperate in skill-building around it. Knowing the topic ahead of time enables them to reflect on what they want to say, and a common focus helps them clarify and remember their conclusions.

Weighed against these benefits is the value of free association. Their minds may not wish to go A-B-C, but rather A-G-Z, surfacing what matters to them but by an unforeseeable route. Either way, with a teacher's competent moderating, open discussions can have a powerful effect. Although you may begin with a selected topic, listen for divergent comments and allow participants to decide if they want to follow them out. Select topics in several ways.

Topic Areas

Fill the writing board with topics they would like to talk about (or refer them to the lists in the Appendix). They can then go to the board and make tally marks beside the ten they personally prefer. Doing the tallying in writing, instead, gives everyone cover from revealing their worries publicly and prevents any students from dominating. They hand in their preferences for you to add up.

Many topics are important for addressing fears, unfamiliar situations, and pending issues. A topic's urgency to them may be far beyond their ability to think it through, such as middle school students wanting to discuss boy-girl relationships. It may help to have more than one topic available and know they can return to significant ones as they discover more they can say. Make up a list all agree on, post it, and schedule topics accordingly.

One direction is to ask them questions like the first set listed in 26, Life Knowledge, without providing an answer. They figure out theirs, you add in your own or the book's, and together devise a comprehensive version.

The Appendix contains several lists with wide age relevance and challenge. Students can nominate from these lists and either reach consensus by discussion or vote for those that they want.

When they are fluid at developing thoughts together, try out advanced topics that have multiple meanings and metaphorical associations for them to explore (Appendix 5). Arrange groups. Ask one student to pick one for the class by touching the list with a pencil with his eyes closed. He announces it and the groups start. To work regularly with these, duplicate Appendix 5, cut it into as many equal pieces as you have students, and let them write each topic on separate slips of paper you collect in a sack. When you announce groups, draw a topic randomly.

Spontaneity and prior reflection emphasize different skills. Sometimes preparing for discussion can encourage deeper thought. A day ahead, ask them to write out their thoughts about the topic and bring them to their group. Everyone shares what they have written so that each one's ideas are accepted before discussing any of them, moderating the influence of dominant students. You might also have them prepare comments, but then use their skills spontaneously as ideas come to their minds. The rough form of a haphazard grade school discussion should morph through the years into a thoroughly prepared postgraduate seminar.

The seven questions given here can help them explore a topic. They might keep the list handy to refer to during small group discussions. Because it is likely to be useful to them throughout their lives, have them master it as a Learning Feat.

1. What is your first thought on hearing the topic? Draw on free association, inviting their initial mental pictures or memories. This alerts everyone to similarities and differences and opens tangents for examination. To accustom them to having a first thought, suggest that they notice how they start thinking about it, catch what comes up first. You might use the list of advanced topics (Appendix 5) to practice: Announce one, wait a few seconds, and do a Consult (cf. 21) on the very first thought, word, or picture that arises in each one's mind. Do this rapidly on several occasions until everyone grasps having a first thought.
2. What experience have you had about the topic? What have they lived through that relates to the topic?
3. What feelings does the topic bring up? Hearing their feelings in response to the topic expands social and emotional learning. They need rich and detailed knowledge about how issues affect others.
4. What different meanings does the topic have? Explore literal, figurative, and metaphorical meanings. Mountain can refer to a topographical feature, a challenge in one's life, or what one makes from a molehill. Unfolding the meaning of a topic is the work of discussion.
5. What is most important to you about the topic? Explore how it could impact their lives or connect them with others.
6. Do you have a question related to the topic? Topics are often important because of how their unknowns may affect us and so are often incomplete or unclear. Let students think what they want to discover.
7. What action can you foresee that relates to the topic? Though it may be far in the future, they may make their first choice about it in your classroom.

15. DISCUSSION GROUPS

We manage discussions intensively to accomplish more in less time and guide students as they deal with unfamiliar behaviors.

1. Form groups. Form groups of three to six students. The more participants in each, the greater the competition for talking time so the better must be the communication skills. Although younger children need

larger numbers in an adult-led group, four or five in a group is a good starting number for most classes, with two or three in the primary grades. Invite them to cluster with others sitting nearby, but modify groups quickly for those who either don't get along or could help each other better.

2. Choose a topic. Explain reasons for selecting a topic, and generate a list from which they draw one for the day. For variety, you might also announce "No topic today" so they can practice developing ideas spontaneously. The seven questions previously given for exploring topics can help them enter the discussion while their confidence grows. As they relax, they need fewer suggestions.
3. Plan skill use. We want them respectfully developing ideas others offer. To achieve this, they choose skills from the CSCS, and check their use afterward. Explain any skill you especially want them to practice (cf. 11).
4. Set a time limit and run it. Keep the time short to start. When they can include everyone during an eight-minute discussion with good skills, consider extending it. Eventually they may use a full period productively, but early on intervene right away if the activity deteriorates.
5. Check their skills. Use the CSCS for feedback after the discussion (cf. 11). They can alternate rating themselves or someone else on their use of the skills.
6. Verbal feedback. Once they know what the skills are, growth lies in the choice to use them. Their comments to each other powerfully influence this decision.
7. Recall of content. Expecting to recall the content later alerts them to it during the discussion. One way is to divide them into pairs and tell back "who said what," or "everything said in the group," or "a summary of the discussion," or "the most important points." One partner can attempt the whole narrative, switching on alternate days, or they can each take half the time. In two minutes they readily summarize what they want to retain. There is no better way to install an insight than to remember others' specific comments about it. They have more relevance than bare generalizations.
8. Write questions and answers. Writing sustains insights but takes more time. Use it when the content is academic or when their conclusions could be valuable to them later. You might ask them to (1) identify the question(s) their discussion answered, (2) write the question on the Questions page of the appropriate notebook section and (3) write the answer in the Answers section. They could (4) work together to summarize an ideal answer, (5) include some of each student's sharing in it, and (6) let everyone copy the result.

9. Managing discussions. If a student hinders the group, place that student a little back from it but close enough to hear. Say, "Watch what they're doing until you get the hang of it." The student makes this adjustment best when he or she has nothing else to do but observe others' model of cooperation while still feeling connected to the group. A location half in and half out appears to serve best. When the student says he or she understands, return the student to the group.

Let their level of confidence guide you in how many days to leave groups intact. Withdrawn students may need longer to get comfortable. If they are confident and communicate easily, the stimulation of shifting membership even daily may suit them better. In general, build trust and safety before versatility. Let them gain ease talking in one group before changing groups.

These four rules generate a discussion, but debriefing afterward enhances its quality. Use no more than two of steps five to eight on any day; one of either five or six, and/or one of either seven or eight. The first pair reinforce the development of the process, and the second the assimilation of the content. Knowing that later they can rate skills, give feedback, remember, or summarize the discussion gives them a reason to pay better attention.

For the one receiving it, a smile, a reference to their contribution to the group, or a phrase describing a skill they used adds to their self-understanding and confidence: "You asked a question that helped draw out his idea," "You helped her tell about her feeling," or "You gave a really clear example." Invite them to note each person's contribution, and how someone used a skill toward them. Even a minute of this after a discussion makes a difference.

Observe what occurs. The noise level when you see everyone participating and enjoying it sounds like a high hum—light, without brassy exclamations, raucous laughter, or putdowns that might cause some to withdraw. Note body position. When people are interested, they usually lean forward to hear better. Groups become more compact. As you see body position spreading out or turning aside, group connection is weakening. Do they look at the speaker?

Note facial expression, preferably animated, mobile, and changing congruently with the flow of meaning. As it dulls to a mask-like appearance or eyelids droop, they are losing energy.

Listen in: Are they still on the subject, reflecting more deeply, using words accurately or superficially? If they might benefit from continuing, ask them quietly, "Are you done or do you want more time?" Ideally, you want them so immersed in their discussion that they fail to hear you.

16. CONFLICT RESOLUTION

At the African-American Academy (cf. Chapter 1), Mr. Dawson caught me excitedly one day as I walked in. He indicated a boy in the far corner of the room.

"He's been one of the worst in starting fights on the playground," he said. "Hardly a day would go by without a fight." I glanced at the boy. In class he had participated like the others in communication skills practice, feelings discussions, and Learning Feats.

"Today the boys were playing a game outside during lunchtime," the teacher continued. "They got into an argument and were shouting at each other. I went over closer because that kind of thing would always break down into fighting before. This time I heard him reflect back what the other was saying, 'So you're saying that . . .' and the other student picked it up and they started talking about it. And in a few minutes they solved it and were back playing the game!" He grinned broadly. It had been a tough year for them to that point.

If your class needs extra practice in conflict resolution, select skills from the CSCS or from the two lists given here. Demonstrate them and add others as a Learning Feat. The Content Scoreboard (cf. 47) can help students track their mastery of the skills.

Give seven skills for solving conflicts.

1. Feel respect and consideration.
2. Ask questions.
3. Ask about their feelings.
4. Describe what affects you.
5. Check out your guesses about others' thoughts and feelings.
6. Summarize others' thoughts and feelings.
7. Talk out problems.

Give five steps for talking out problems.[8]

1. What is the problem? (State it so it includes how everyone sees it.)
2. What have we tried? (What previous efforts tried to solve it?)
3. How did they work? (Identify results so far and reflect on them).
4. What else can we try? (Involve everyone in expanding options.)
5. What will we do next? (Agree on a next step that works for all.)

17. USE RATINGS

We continue a process as we keep in mind a reason for doing so. Noticing a different reason leads us to a different activity. This implies that for students to change, we need to make them conscious of a reason and help them focus on the outcome of applying it.

Rating a quality of the classroom is one way to do this. A classroom quality is relevant because it affects their experience.

Rate You

You can begin by asking them to rate your listening ability. Say

> I want to improve my listening. At the end of the day, I'll give you a blank slip of paper. Write on it a number from zero to ten and turn it in. Ten would mean I listened almost perfectly to you, I understood your feelings, your needs, and your ideas very well. Five means I was so-so in listening, and zero means I didn't listen at all.

Pay attention then to how you listen. Repeat back their ideas to clarify what they mean. Look at them when they speak, move closer, adjust your voice tone and pace to theirs, lower your eye level to match theirs, and follow their train of thought. Then at the end of the day, invite them to tell what they observed about your listening. Let their written ratings be anonymous because they may also reflect how they feel about you or the class in general.

Post the average in a box you draw on the writing board or list it by dates. When you have several, make a line chart and plot your scores proceeding upward across it (assuming they see you improving). They will note that this appears interesting and achievable, a map they can follow.

Rate Class Overall

Identify classroom qualities they can influence and ask them to rate the measures selected 0–10. If you have already demonstrated listening and had them practice it, you might start with how well others listened to them. Cut scratch paper into small squares and distribute them before the close of class. They do the rating and drop the slips in a jar as they leave. Five others are:

How well did I support others? On alternate days you can switch to How well did others support me? Charting their respective answers, such as with different colored lines on the same chart, can stimulate discussion and remind them of changes they might make. If they rate themselves as supporting others at 8 and receiving support at 4, the difference deserves discussion.

Maybe they need more Appreciation Time or examining how people perceive the same thing differently. Rating can awaken them to attitudes of accepting, helping, and being kind to each other. Enlist a student volunteer to add, average, and post class scores. You can also place a dot above and below the average to mark the highest and lowest scores reported.

How much effort did I expend? (How hard did I try?) Discuss concentration, mood variances, complacency, staying on task, and restoring their enthusiasm.

How well did we take charge of our learning? Ask students to measure themselves on this when they undertake classroom organization teams (cf. 18). The more methods in learning, memory, and cooperation they can use independently, the higher this score can be.

How interesting did we make learning today? This question presumes that students have some independence and can help design their own learning.

Without telling them your intent to evaluate the design explained here, you can also ask them to measure factors for which staff collects baseline data (cf. Chapter 9). Conscious self-rating is part of the design. They are encouraged by knowing that the number of fights or the amount of litter has declined.

The Progress Ladder (Appendix 8) integrates several continua marking students' growing maturity, self-direction, and emotional balance. They typically enjoy estimating their progress from one category to another. Make a copy for them to insert in their notebooks, and ask them to score themselves weekly. Most do so fairly accurately, but if you notice a rating unrealistically high or low, discuss it with the student: "What features of this combined rating do you think you are strong or weak in?" Invite them to underline or star specific sentences that represent their next step of development.

18. ORGANIZATION GROUPS

Students acquire individual responsibility easiest in small groups directing their own efforts. They show they are ready for this by their progress in acceptance, communications, and giving good feelings to each other. Academic and developmental purposes align as they experience inclusion and influence by means of learning itself.

Designing the Groups

For organization groups to aid students' learning and development, their composition matters more than with discussion groups reconfigured frequently. Members need to help each other, not irritate others, and support the one who most needs it. Random drawing of groups or free choice can load one with problems while others burst with talent.

Students can help you design the best experience for those you worry about. First, everyone writes their name at the top of a piece of paper and draws a line down the middle. One side they title Be With, where they list those with whom they would like to be in a group. They title the other Learn From and list those they think they could best learn from. The first elicits liking and the second respect—two qualities contributing to a positive group experience.

Leave it up to them if they ask, "How many can we name?" The more they name, the more connected they are, and the more likely to be the bridging person you want to find. Assure them that you are the only one who will see their list, and ask them not to talk about their nominations.

When you are alone, make up a spreadsheet with namers down the left and the same list across the top as namees to identify who selected whom. Take one student's sheet at a time. Note his or her name at the top, and go to that person listed down the left side of your spreadsheet. To the right, place a tally under each of those he or she lists.

When you have done all of them, total up the nominations. Identify first those named least. They have the fewest tallies under their names. Few chose them to be with or learn from. These are the class rejects, the nervous ones who expect hurts from others, the socially awkward, fearful, and shy. Go to their row and check the names of others whom they tallied, and among that group find the ones named most. These are the bridging people, the ones they like who are also popular with others. Give them their top choices of those students, especially if they were chosen in return. You want to place the most needing students with others with whom they immediately experience harmony. Assign the remainder to balance ability and cooperation and to respect their choices where possible.

Assign captains. Among those you regard as the best leaders, note which are named most by students, and combine the group's judgment with your own. Call them whatever fits their frame of reference: captain, big beetle, alpha dog, admiral. Expand the meaning of their role by asking them to find in their social studies how organizations designate leaders and what they do. Suggest a mission for them such as "to assure learning and harmony in my group." Teach them actions they can do right away and consult with them regularly on their progress:

Helping their group organize materials and notebooks.

Assigning daily practice partners within their group.
Dividing up projects or assignments, giving each a part to do.
Monitoring the accuracy of their members' scores in time and points.
Adding up and posting members' scores on class scoreboards.
Suggesting ways of rating their group's progress.
Reporting results to you.
Solving problems that arise between group members.
Thinking of ways to increase interest in learning.
Receiving supplies from a class Supplies Captain and accounting for them.
Signing out their group to the library or for other special projects.
Being accountable for their behavior.
Cooperating with other group captains on projects or study.

Add responsibilities until their group works as an independent unit. Make the captains a team to run the classroom all the ways they can, and suggest that they apply to their group the model you use with them: Ask people to do what they can and back them up.

Be ready to intervene early. Each student needs first to find a place, an experience of acceptance. Until this happens, learning is impaired for the one not accepted. Divert ineffective strategies: "Joe, I noticed that you (did such and such), and then . . . happened. Would you like to try something that might work better? What can you think of doing differently? Here's a suggestion."

If clashes occur in the first groups, do what is easiest for the most vulnerable. The deeper their personal needs, the more important it is to build support around them. If you must move someone, choose someone else. They have already experienced not fitting in and this is just one more hurt. Move others instead who are flexible—the constructive closer and the destructive further away—and try to leave target students where they find reassurance.

How long to maintain group composition depends on their needs and your goals. Entering a different group, they practice establishing themselves with new people, yet you also want their productivity in clicking as a team. A middle ground is probably between two and four weeks. After three weeks, you might be guided by having them write what they learned from being in their group. Sometimes you can shift leaders in the same group; appoint them yourself while hearing the captain's recommendation for a successor, or let the first leader select and train a lieutenant who takes over next. How they change leaders can occasion a discussion of such roles in family and society.

Three ways to use the groups for learning are for discussions, dividing subjects (cf. 43), and paired work. Groups of four provide each person with three others to partner with, balancing variety with continuity and support.

Chapter Four

Teach Self-Management

Students' attitudes affect how they learn and relate to others. Teachers can influence them through direct contact, teaching self-management skills, and arranging for students to influence each other's feelings and behavior (cf. 9).

19. APPRECIATION LIST

Any of us can verify the lasting power of appreciation by recalling when we received it ourselves. An example is a story circulated on the Internet without attribution that I pass on as received:

> One day, a teacher asked her students to list the names of the other students in the classroom on a sheet of paper, leaving a space between each name. Then, she told them to think of the nicest thing about each of their classmates and write it down. It took the remainder of the class period to finish this assignment, and as the students left the room, they handed in their paper. That Saturday, the teacher wrote down the name of each student on a separate sheet of paper and listed what everyone else had said about them.
>
> On Monday, she gave them all their list. Before long, the entire class was smiling. "Really?" she heard whispered. "I never knew that I meant anything to anyone!" and "I didn't know others liked me so much," were most of the comments. No one ever mentioned those papers in class again. She never knew if they discussed them after class or with their parents, but it didn't matter. The exercise had accomplished its purpose. The students were happy with themselves and one another, and that group moved on.
>
> Several years later, one of the students was killed in Vietnam, and this teacher attended his funeral. She had never seen a serviceman in a military coffin before. He looked so handsome, so mature. The church was packed with his

friends. One by one, those who loved him took a last walk by his coffin. The teacher was the last one to bless the coffin. As she stood there, one of the soldiers who acted as pallbearer came up to her.

"Were you Mark's high school math teacher?" he asked.

"Yes," she nodded.

"Mark talked about you a lot," the soldier said. After the funeral, most of Mark's former classmates went together to a luncheon. Mark's mother and father were there, obviously waiting to speak with this teacher.

"We want to show you something," his father said, taking a wallet out of his pocket. 'They found this on Mark when he was killed. We thought you might recognize it." Opening the billfold, he carefully removed two worn pieces of notebook paper that had obviously been taped, folded, and refolded many times. The teacher knew without looking that the papers were the ones on which she had listed all the good things each of Mark's classmates had said about him.

"Thank you so much for doing that," Mark's mother said. "As you can see, Mark treasured it." All of Mark's former classmates started to gather around. Charlie smiled rather sheepishly and said, "I still have my list. It's in the top drawer of my desk at home." Chuck's wife said, "Chuck asked me to put his in our wedding album." "I have mine too," Marilyn said. "It's in my diary." Then Vicki, another classmate, reached into her pocketbook, took out her wallet and showed her worn and frazzled list to the group. "I carry this with me at all times," Vicki said, and without batting an eyelash continued, "I think we all saved our lists."

The teacher sat down and cried. She cried for Mark and for all his friends who would never see him again . . . we forget that life will end one day. And we don't know when that one day will be . . .

Your personal feedback can impact a student: "I've been thinking about what you did in class the other day, and I wanted to mention that it stood out in a couple ways. . . ." This implies to the student that: (1) you were worth thinking about, (2) I looked deeper into you, and (3) found positive meaning. Your message is more believable as it arises from genuine reflection. Their outer accomplishment has passed and a more personal thought arrives. People treasure discernment that lets them know they are truly seen and that what is seen is valued.

20. FINDING GOOD

Students' unacceptable behavior may shake our balance. We disapprove and are tempted toward negative comments. We realize that we may alienate them and make their misbehavior more likely, yet if we ignore it and suppress our antipathy, they may think we cave in. We want them to know that we are on their side even if we must discipline them.

We accomplish this by offering an accurate but positive perception of the student's negative behavior. We look deeper into the negative to find a positive in it. We don't excuse it or ignore the need for a consequence but rather say, "I see good in you even though your use of it is against our rules." A quality in the student is either neutral at worst or fundamentally good that we can respect. Once acknowledging that, we deal better with its improper use.

Each situation given here might prompt a ten-minute problem-solving conversation with the student. You want to generate understanding while sustaining the bridge between you.

1. A student talks to other students while you talk, diverting from the subject and distracting others. You are frustrated and annoyed. In the past you may have made a comment to the student that he or she resents.

Talking to others is an innate, constructive human activity. Through it we connect to others and meet our needs. After class you might face the student and say, "Jerome, I notice that you like to talk to people. This is a good thing you'll do for the rest of your life. It's important to be able to connect with people around us. People express their friendship and help each other when they talk. The problem is that doing it during class while I try to explain something makes it harder for you and everyone to listen and follow. Do you understand the problem?

"So I'd like to ask you to notice the feeling of wanting to talk. When that feeling comes up, tell yourself that you can do it later. Would you try that? Try to sense the desire coming up inside you before you say something. Instead of talking then, save what you want to say for later. Tomorrow I'll ask you if you experienced that desire and how you handled it."

2. A student's sarcastic comment about another student makes others laugh. Because you hate to see anyone hurt, this upsets you and your first instinct is to level the one who made the comment.

Look for the positive within the negative, such as: "Aaron, you have an ability I respect. I think it will help you throughout your life. It's your feel for words. Sometimes you can find a word that expresses perfectly what you want to say, and this will be a big asset to you. All your life it may help you make others laugh.

"What's not acceptable here, though, is that your humor can make someone feel bad. That makes it not worth it. Getting a laugh by making someone feel bad tends to come back on us eventually and drives good people away from us. They may laugh, but they know that someone is hurt, so they feel unsafe around you. Can we think of ways you can use your ability with words and your sense of humor, maybe for your next writing assignment?"

3. A student gets very emotional and calls another student names. The incident was blown out of proportion and you cannot think of any positive element in it.

The student before you has emotional presence, a capacity or power that can be used for good or ill. If you want to see it used for good, you first acknowledge its existence. You might say, "Angela, one thing I notice about you that can be a strength in the future is that you have emotional presence. You are really here wherever you are. Whether you are feeling up or down, people sense it and they can feel in touch with you because you have reserves of emotion that connect to them automatically.

"Good leaders often have this capacity and they guide it so that it helps others. You might not even notice the power of your feelings. Often when we are upset we can't tell how they affect others. What's not acceptable here is blame and anger toward others. If there is a problem between you and someone else, we want you to explain it to a teacher and then it's up to us what to do next.

"You can help by noticing a feeling starting to rise inside you. Usually you become very aware of it before you express it in words. Could you and I check a couple times a day about how feelings rise and how you handle them?"

4. A bright student tends to get the day's lesson quickly but then spaces out and draws pictures and ignores much of what occurs in class. The negative is nonattention to the lesson, distracting others, and the model this provides to others to do the same. The positive is the student's quickness of mind and possible creative ability. Often keen thinkers are impelled to reorganize what comes to them so that they find routine difficult. You might say, "Kevin, I appreciate about you that I can count on you to understand what I explain. You have a quick mind that will serve you well. But it misleads other students to see you divert from what we do in class. It leads others in that direction. Do you see the problem? We need to figure out how to put your mind to work. Maybe you can reoutline the lesson or go on to the next one, or we can arrange other things for you."

You identify the root capacity involved and find in yourself genuine respect for it. You express this to the student, identify its improper use and outcomes, project possibilities for its positive use, and note the consequences you foresee. Following are other situations along with a couple sentences that express a viewpoint to take:

A student fights: "You're not afraid of physical encounters. You have evidently overcome your fear of being hurt yourself."

A student criticizes others: "You see that others could behave better. You see how they could improve."

A student pushes others around: "You have physical strength and assertiveness."

A student comes late to everything: "You have your own clock, your own sense of timing and action."

A student ignores school rules, coming and going as she pleases: "You are able to be independent, to stand aside from usual rules."

A student lies: "A lie helps you avoid something unpleasant or gain a benefit. You can imagine what might harm you."

A student gathers a clique that rejects others: "You can make intense connections with a few people and are loyal to your friends."

A student is so quiet she never says anything: "You're very easy to get along with. You're a calming influence."

A student persists in negative behavior despite attempts to get him to change: "You have persistence in following out your own idea. You can stick to something you want to do."

A student steals from another's locker: "You can make a plan and carry it out." If the action was instead impulsive, your comment might be, "You can see what looks like an opportunity and jump into it quickly. You're a quick responder."

A student is competitive and cannot tolerate anyone else winning: "You have a drive to excel."

A student distracts the class with comic gestures and motions. "You can make people laugh."

This approach sustains our link with the student by conveying respect and avoiding words with negative implications or a critical tone. We are objective and straightforward, saying nothing a student must defend against. He or she does not wince from a subtle dig but receives accurate information pro and con about the action.

A fundamental balance makes the approach work. On the one hand, we gain credibility by accurately acknowledging the negative aspects of the student's behavior, which in turn makes our positive comments also believable. This practice can bridge even to students who seem to try deliberately to appear at their worst. Many wish desperately to be respected but feel driven to find out what others think of them. If their misdeed loosens a condemnation from a teacher, it was worth it to get into trouble to find out. If, on the other hand, the teacher finds a basis of respect, they gain a tiny purchase on a better view of themselves.

Note that the approach does not change the subject. If we address a student's sarcasm, it is a diversion to say, "You're physically strong." Though true, it leaves hanging the question of what we think of his sarcasm.

Search out the helpful shred within the objectionable behavior: "So you felt that he was backing you up" or "It made you feel strong for that time" or "You felt really original." We want access to their thinking about their behavior and open it by finding a positive element and respecting it. As we need to, we say, "But do you see the flaw in that?", "On the other hand, someone was injured, weren't they?", "You excluded someone and hurt their feelings," or "You knew that was against school rules, right?"

If students exhibit a negative attitude in front of you, they invite you to grapple with it. They want you to draw on your best thoughts and consider their ideas. Those we most want to reach believe that something in them is so bad they can't even talk about it with a respectable person, so they reveal it tangentially. The negativity they feel temporarily at first can gradually take over and pervade their moods permanently.

Think of their need to realize the good about themselves and compare it to what we know about juvenile corrections. The sheer time young people spend "in the system" correlates best with how much more crime they engage in later. The more "correction" they receive, the worse they get. How could this be?

Certainly the worse their behavior, the longer their initial sentence. But the longer time an experience channels their thinking, the more completely it fills in a picture of themselves. If everywhere around them they see a maladaptive plan, when they select their actions, they have only maladaptive plans to choose from.

Reminders of their strengths and even their small good intentions help redesign their picture. Their minds may be so oppressed by negative experience that they do not know how to be positive even mentally and must leave it to you where to place the key. If you can tease out a positive from what they say, they appreciate it. And as you deal objectively with it, they note that this is fitting and are more likely to accept your direction. As they feel better by applying the direction you suggest, they are more likely to continue in it.

To convey such learning, you might pass on your observation of cause and effect in one-liners, summarizing briefly their behavior and its outcome:

You listened and felt connected.
You paid attention and got into the work easier.
You took a chance and had more fun.
You remembered and others valued that.
You thought it through and figured it out.

21. STUDY FEELINGS

Many commercial programs offer approaches to affective development. The need for addressing this zone is well understood.[9] We would like to make all students expert in managing it. Besides the means suggested in other sections, some are simple and basic:

1. Vocabulary. We enter the inner zone first by naming it accurately. A body of knowledge opens as we become familiar with its vocabulary.

Pick out feelings you identify as important or let your students select them (cf. Appendix 1). Then just understand what each feeling means. Name one, ask a student to look it up and share the definition with the class, and invite experiences with it. Ask them to watch for the feeling as the day unfolds (prompting them to manage their feelings all day), and report later. You (1) identify a feeling, (2) offer a perspective on it, (3) ask them to note when it occurs, and (4) do a Consult (cf. below) at the day's end about their observations.

Clustering feelings aids understanding. Students must think about the meaning of each one and the differences between them. Pick out twenty and ask pairs or teams to talk out how they would group them as pleasant, unpleasant, brief, long-lasting, important, or unimportant; or by how they isolate or connect people or how they reflect positive or negative feelings about oneself. Discriminating their meaning helps students manage them more consciously.

2. Class discussion. For talking about their personal concerns, the appendices offer many topics, or your class can develop and prioritize its own list. Note the progression of the questions here from general and impersonal to specific and immediate.

What things generally give people good feelings?[10]
Name all the ways students can give others good feelings.
What does it mean to be a friend?
How do people show they are friendly?
How many friends can a person have?
Are there different kinds of friends?
How can people be kind and helpful at school?
What things usually give you a good feeling?
What things about school give you a good feeling?
How do good feelings affect you differently than bad feelings?
How does it affect you when people are friendly?
Name something you have at home that gives you a good feeling.
Tell about a time recently when someone gave you a good feeling.

How could I give you a good feeling?

3. Assignments. Analyze how historical events were impelled by emotions such as love, hate, greed, hubris, resentment, confidence, fear, and optimism. Use the theme for writing assignments and interpreting current events.

4. The Consult. The Consult (accent the first syllable) helps you discover their prevailing mood, unify their focus, and initiate a discussion. Use it at the beginning of a period to gain their attention, or following an outburst in class, a playground problem, a school event, a learning performance, a public calamity, or one person's experience that has meaning for others. It may have provoked an emotional reaction, could be viewed from several angles, or reminded them of a personal experience.

To employ it, ask one question everyone can answer in a single word or phrase, such as:

What did you feel when (the event) happened?
What are you feeling now about it?
What thought came to your mind when (the event) happened?
What do you think about it now?
What word summarizes that experience for you?

Wait briefly while everyone formulates their answer. Tell them you will hear each before discussing any, and then invite their word, phrase, or sentence. Engage them afterward about any dominant theme or significant incident they express.

5. Start the day. Their habitual, subjective world comes face to face in the morning with the larger objective world the classroom represents. You might use a Consult then by saying, "Give one word about your current feeling." Notice if any share a feeling that could hinder learning. Who is sad, discouraged, mad, upset, or tense? Listen to the experience attached to the feeling, affirm an aspect of what the student shared, and understand how causes played out.

If needed, problem solve by talking out an action, making an appointment, or selecting a topic for later discussion. Knowing their place is secure and affirmed, and that their problem is being managed, they can better invest in the current activity: "Well then, is everyone ready to go to work?" If they have a feeling they don't want to expose to the class but would like it considered, let them suggest it privately to you as a topic for discussion.

6. Use unplanned experiences. Unscheduled "targets of opportunity" can beg for a response.

One day my students went out for recess into moist snow. A snowball fight erupted. Later I noted unhappy expressions: aggrieved, vengeful, and defensive. A few believed others had "ganged up" on them and some were observers. Several issues invited resolution.

A superb discussion followed in which the aggrieved stated their case, observers supplied information, those responsible for injury admitted their excesses and apologized, and the group together created guidelines that modified later snowball fights.

Such experiences offer easy success: Have your basket ready in case they shake the tree. At some point during the year, an event is likely to occur that touches everyone, and all will have a point to relate—a deed they observed, a perception to verify, or a feeling to note—and all will be open to hearing from everyone. If your class lives an untroubled existence, you may even plan an occasional group experience likely to test them by generating meaningful material. Prepare your plan. *Carpe diem.*

7. Affirmation activities. Many activities approached playfully can help even older students grasp the reality of their feelings.

They might (1) name a feeling or a common experience that evokes a feeling (e.g., petting your cat) and count how many students have had it. (2) How pleasant was it? (Little ones can raise their hand above ground to show how "high" the feeling was). (3) How intense? (Arms hugging self tightly or loosely). (4) How long in duration? (Arms extended little or much to either side, fingers pointing away.) (5) Cut out pictures from magazines and discuss what the person might be feeling. (6) If their name were a feeling, what would their name be? They make a nametag for themselves that expresses their feeling of the day and wear it. (7) Make a pie with each slice representing how much of different feelings they carry around (usually, or right then). Change the size of the pieces as needed. (8) Search around inside. What do they find there? (9) Shift deliberately between three kinds of feelings. If they experience an unhappy one from time to time, let them try to change it to feeling happy and then peaceful. With a negative experience, it is enough to sense just the edge of the feeling without immersing themselves in it, and then move their attention to the positive ones. Help them notice how they change inside as they shift their focus. (10) Let's celebrate someone today. Be free to ask to be celebrated. (11) Discuss what to do if they think someone gives them a bad feeling. Do they have to accept such a gift?

8. Go for it. One teacher had an hour a week with middle school students assigned to her because of their problem behavior and moderated a discussion about managing feelings and communication skills. She also expected them to absorb everything, concluding each session by asking, "Okay, who's ready to go for it?" A student summarized the

entire hour's discussion, incorporating everyone's contribution. They all could do this, she said, a notable achievement causing everyone to weigh their own words carefully and absorb others' ideas better. By the end of the year their problems had disappeared.

9. Questions about feelings. The questions here are a way for students to connect one to one with others whom they want to understand or help. Have them learn the questions in order as a Learning Feat. Suggest that they ask them of someone outside the class and report what happens:

    1. What do you feel now?
    2. Did the feeling come from inside or outside?
    3. What happened to make you feel that?
    4. Have you had the feeling before?
    5. What happened then?
    6. What else did you feel then?
    7. What did you think then?
    8. Have you tried to change it before?
    9. How can you help change the feeling now?
    10. What choices do you have?
    11. How can I help?

The questions follow three themes: (1) the nature of one's feelings, (2) the sources of and associations with them, and (3) how one expects to manage them.

22. BREATHE FOR CALMING

We take our breathing for granted as it goes in and out irregularly. Making it even and regular takes conscious focus. The moment our attention wanders, old rhythms resume. Because of its reliance on continuous attention, breathing evenly frees our mind from habitual worries and distractions, stabilizes the body, calms the mind, and increases oxygen intake.

Ask students to breathe at exactly the same rate in and out for a few minutes. A gauge placed at their mouth or nose would record constant liters of air per minute passing that point. Ask them to monitor their level of inner calm and assign it a 0–10 score with the latter the calmest. They will notice their inner world steadily more serene.

Quiet humming helps by increasing nitric oxide in the sinus cavities, reducing susceptibility to infection and increasing blood flow in the capillaries of the brain for numerous benefits to learning.[11] Aid students further by asking them to close their eyes, sit erect and balanced to minimize body tension, and bring a single calming image before their mind.

Few activities done together for three to five minutes are as universally centering as steady breathing, humming, and a calming image.

23. UNDERSTAND CAUSALITY

We can think of students' energy as flowing in rivers, streams, and rivulets. Usually we can divert the rivulets with requests, consequences, and rewards. The rivers of their energy are so substantial that students typically change only through personal insight and sustained choice. Because emotions comprise much of this energy, we need to help students understand and direct them.

Emotional experience contains microsteps when choice is possible: (1) the preexisting situation, (2) causes or triggers of the feeling, (3) its internal effects and sensations, (4) how the student handled it, and (5) the outcomes.

Select a feeling important to your students, positive or negative. Choose it yourself (such as embarrassment) or help them do so (cf. Appendix 1). Write the feeling at the top center of the writing board, create five wide columns, and from the left title them "Situation," "Causes," "Effects," "Choices," and "Outcomes." Ask students to make their own chart on a sheet of paper for personal study. Questions for each stage generate insight though you may not have time for them all. A few generate an overview you can develop later.

Invite four to six students to share one experience with the selected feeling. Tell them you will track it across all the stages by their answers, summarizing their words a column at a time. You would hear from volunteers first about the location and setting they were in when the feeling occurred, jotting their comments briefly in the first column. Filling in one column with all of them together and moving to the next creates a sense of advancing a common frontier of knowledge.

Place students' comments about subsequent stages beside theirs at a previous one. While you work on the board with four, invite the class to apply the template to themselves, filling in the columns on their sheet with their own experience with the feeling:

Situation

In this column jot their description of where they were just before the feeling was triggered.

Where were you (physical location)?
What were you expecting or wanting?
Was there a setup likely to produce the feeling?
Were you with people who influence you?
Was there already a positive or negative feeling?
If so, was it strong or weak?

The point here is that a setting can generate a feeling, so choosing where they go is their first leverage over their feeling.

Causes

Write what elicited or sparked the feeling.

What choices did you make just before the feeling came on?
What trigger spurred the feeling, such as a word, deed, or event?
Did you foresee that this would happen?
Did you allow others to influence you?

Discuss how individuals react differently to the same trigger. They can choose to change how they receive it or can let it sail past them. A student might say about a negative trigger, "I just think 'Cancel!' when I hear that." For external causes to affect them, they must consent. They can head off a feeling if they want to, which is the second point for making a change.

Effects

After they have reacted to the trigger and allowed the feeling to begin inside them, impacts that seem spontaneous affect their mind and body.

What were your first reactions?
What did you do and say that felt automatic?
What images and thoughts came up?
What did they remind you of?
What feelings and body sensations came up?
How strong were the sensations and how long did they last?
Did the event replay old feelings or experiences?
Could you influence the strength of any feelings or sensations?

The key learning is that their prior choices may immerse them in an inner experience still partly under their control that they can expand or minimize. They can catastrophize it or place it in perspective—their third occasion for managing it.

Choices

Conscious behavioral selections cope with or steer their experience after the feeling occurred and after they noticed its inner effects.

How deliberate were your choices?
At the time, did you think your choice was the right one?
How long did you think about what to do?
Did you consider long-term outcomes or just short-term ones?
Did you pause to think about others or think only about yourself?
What did you choose to do?

Here they decide to express, manage inwardly, or moderate their feeling, constituting their fourth point of leverage for change.

Outcomes

Finally, note the results of the different ways students managed their experience:

Were the outcomes positive or negative? (Write a large + or – beside each experience you tracked.)
What did you and others think, do, and feel?
If the feeling was negative, how did you get past it?
What did you learn?
What is your feeling now about the experience?
How do you wish you had handled it?

This last look at their experience is their fifth occasion for exerting control when they may rethink what to do later in a similar situation.

The steps can bring a seemingly reflex response under deliberate management. As they learn to foresee the progression of an event, they can choose whether to allow its steps to occur as they appear headed or redirect them. Discussing the stages in small groups can deepen their understanding. Make a handout of the five stages for their personal use.

24. SELF-CORRECTION

A set of thoughts propels any way we repeatedly act unproductively. We change the action by changing how we instruct ourselves.

Ask students to draw a line down the middle of a sheet of paper. Title the left "Old" and the right "New." On the left, ask them to list all their thoughts that come up repeatedly. You would expect an endless list but there appears to be an innate practical maximum of a dozen, give or take a couple. A few thoughts capture the overwhelming majority of the time we spend thinking, recycling our preoccupations, frustrations, hopes, and fears. Often they follow a recurrent feeling. Suggest students identify feelings they have often, and pick out the thought that accompanies each.

Three-quarters or more of your own statements may be positive, like "I love my wife (husband)," or "My kids are great," whereas others focus on difficulties like "This coworker really bugs me," or "How can I increase my income?", or "What am I going to do if X happens?"

It may take students time to compose their list. Start with ten minutes, set the list aside, and return to it the next day. As they reflect on their week, more thoughts usually arise. If they are nosy about what others write, tell everyone you will collect their pages, no one else will see them, and you will hand them back when they work on them next.

When they have written eight or ten in the Old column, look at their list with them individually. They first identify the thoughts already positive and constructive, and write these in the "New" column to save as they are.

The remaining ones that are not constructive or helpful contain the changes they need to make. Help them identify a replacement thought that addresses the same situation but is proactive, realistic, positive, and learning oriented. For example, "I'm worried I'll fail the test" becomes "I get what I've prepared for. I can work harder next time." The feeling of anxiety in the first idea changes to realism and determination. "Barbara is always teasing me and I hate it" turns into "I can let go of what others do." Helplessness and frustration become detachment. "I can't wait till . . ." shifts to "I can focus on what I'm doing now and time will pass faster." Longing becomes patience. The alternate idea applies a different emotional stance to the situation.

They write each improved thought in the New column. They compile all the ideas there into a fluid, connected paragraph, give it a title like My New Life, carry it with them always, and read it at least daily. When an old thought comes up, they are to take out the paragraph, read it thoughtfully; call up its optimism, determination, and realism; and deal with the situation from their strengths instead of their weaknesses.

When they cannot imagine how to replace a negative thought, ask them to pick someone they know who could handle that situation and guess what they would think as they did so. Read your student's old sentence, propose a better one, and ask, "Would this fit? Would this be a good replacement? Could you go to this one instead?" Be sure to address exactly the same situation their old thought addresses. People often try to cope with a problem by turning their mind elsewhere, substituting an unrelated positive one for the negative thought, but this may mean avoiding a problem instead of solving it. Thought patterns unaltered remain ready to sabotage them.

25. RESOURCE STATE

A resource state is a set of capacities enabling us to cope successfully, constructive attitudes linked to practical skills.[12] Confronted with an angry coworker, we want confidence enabling us to listen carefully and respond effectively. If we are criticized, we may need curiosity; if hurried, need balance and a sense of timing; if faced with loss, need acceptance and release. If we are blamed, we want the truthful, problem-solving part to come forward instead of our resentful part. For every situation we face, some aspect of us handles it better than another.

We can help students assemble a general resource state to apply anytime. Tell them, "Today we are going to start building your resource state. We may take several days to finish it. I want you to remember experiences that give you a feeling of strength or competence, as when you play a game and make a score. What is the feeling it gives you?"

When students already feel good, their resource state is typically easy to access. They need it most when it is hardest to obtain—when they are fearful, stressed, or unable to shake negative feelings. To prepare them, we first build an internal state that is neurologically fused and then open an associative trail so they can find it when they need it. We help them open a series of inward doors from one perception to another, quickly remember their competence and confidence, and bypass their maladaptive reactions.

To create the resource state, brainstorm with them a list of productive, positive, personal actions that give them good feelings about themselves. Identify events when they showed competence, understanding of others, determination, confidence, insight, or other abilities. Give a name to each experience and note the trait associated with it. "Accident" might title a moment when they rose to an occasion, knew what to do, and felt confident. "Game" might remind them of a successful sports event. When everyone has several of these resourceful memories identified, ask them to choose five or six covering the resources they want to access later.

Next they join the fragments of feeling and self-image into a unified sense of themselves. Do it by three cues or reminders under their control—a word, an image, and a gesture. Performed together they embed in their physical body a kind of switch that, when thrown, turns on their strengths. The trail opens readily to them if they follow it several times in situations of increasing challenge.

First, they pick the word they want as a name for their overall resource state, a key word unifying their resources. It might be a title designating a specific experience, or just an overall word like "confidence." One woman used "climbing," reminding her how resourceful she felt after a single experience of rock climbing.

Second, they choose an image that appeals to them. It may be of themselves doing a challenging action; or of a physical object, person, or location that gives them a lift; or a symbol they invent.

Finally, they select a gesture like the "okay" symbol with thumb and forefinger in a circle. They use these three together—the word, image, and gesture—solely when they want to remind their brain to refind and call up their resource state and avoid using them unless that is their intent.

When all have identified and named at least five resources and selected their three cues, have them sit quietly, close their eyes, and imagine deeply and vividly the first resource on their list. They call up the feeling they enjoyed when the event first occurred, which is the crucial condition. Ask them to nod their heads silently when they have gained the feeling. When all are in touch with it, ask them to say their key word, bring their key image before their mind, perform their gesture, and enjoy the good feeling briefly.

Do this with each resource separately, and then run through the entire list two or three times until they can just "fire" the three cues and re-experience the good feeling from each resource. Doing this unites the resources into a single state.

To secure and deepen the resource state, for the next several days practice their access to it. Ask them to calm themselves, go within, and return to it using the three cues while reliving the positive memories as needed. Even a few minutes at this can give them confidence that they can restore their resource state when they need it. Note any who may need extra practice with you.

If some say "I don't have any resource experiences," direct their attention to feelings they generate from their own actions: "The best feelings we get come from what we ourselves do. Can you give someone else a good feeling? What needs can you meet? What abilities do you have that are satisfying whenever you do them?" Survey their age-appropriate competences.

You may start some off with positive feedback: "Now close your eyes, listen carefully, and notice what happens inside you when I say something." Pay them a sincere compliment about a strength. The resource they acknowledge is already theirs, but they may not grasp it until you put it into words. If they notice an inward change from hearing your words, tell them, "Well then, we can make that one of your resources. That's what your resource state does. We create it just from the things that give us good feelings about ourselves." Appreciation Time and the CSCS point them to many considerate acts they can perform that are likely to be acknowledged quickly, generating better feelings. Suggest what they can try out, and ask them to check with you daily until they have five they can assemble into a unified resource state.

26. LIFE KNOWLEDGE

As we raise children, we often override their thoughts, feelings, and desires with what we believe is better for them. Our use of "should" says, "You need to set aside what you believe, feel, or think. Do it my way." We substitute our thoughts for theirs to get the conclusion we want, hoping this keeps them safe while they assimilate adult thinking. For a middle school student, the thought "My parents will kill me if I do that" may be enough for the time being.

In the adult world, however, they need to address reality squarely themselves. We want their perceptions to lead them to the best thing whether elders told them or not. They need to examine the world instead of merely what we want of them. We invite them to solve the practical (and moral, relational, familial, economic, and academic) problems it presents: "If you want to be successful later, here is an idea to carve into your brain so you can use it when you need it."

Such knowledge can include all kinds of good advice. Form as question and answer any idea you think is true and important, have them write it in their Miscellaneous notebook section, and score it on the scoreboard as a Learning Feat. With but occasional time spent, you can help them absorb guidelines benefiting them for life. They might apply the ideas to experiences they have, compare different people's views about the answers, or use them as topics for total attention talking time or small group discussion.

You can model answers yourself, and explain how they might have been used during events students know of. The questions vary in complexity but all deserve integration into students' habitual thinking.

1. How do I gain control of my life?

   Make a promise to myself in a small area.
   Keep the promise.
   Extend that to more areas.

2. How long will adults run my life?

   Until I consistently make wise judgments on my own.

3. What are two basic laws at the foundation of our legal system?

   Do all that you agree to do.
   Do not encroach on other persons or their property.[13]

4. When you disagree with someone, what is the first thing to do?

   Try to understand their point of view.

5. What are two questions to ask yourself as you work with others?

   How can I help you?

What can I learn from you?[14]

6. What strengthens your motivation to change?

Having reasons you care about.

7. What trait makes the biggest difference between success and failure?

Persistence.

8. What is the first step to giving others good feelings?

To want them to feel good.

9. What is the main way people become irrational?

They see the world only through their own experience.

10. Name the skills that help most in school.

Listen well.
Give others good feelings.
Remember.

11. How do you become skillful at anything?

Find out what effort pays off.
Practice the effort.

12. What is the hardest but most important thing to do in communications?

Maintain good communications with others while you have intense feelings yourself.

13. What is the first thing to do if you don't like how others treat you?

Notice how you treat them.

14. How can we help ourselves out of pain and hurt?

Recognize that they freeze the mind into mediocre thinking.
Release the pain and hurt.
Find safe people to be with.

15. How do I set standards for myself?

Go beyond what others expect of me.

16. What are four keys to concentration?

Goal: Know what you want to accomplish.
Means: Know where to put your attention to achieve it.
Focus: Ignore everything else while you do that.
Persistence: Keep at it until you reach your goal.

Roots of Behavior

Students need alternatives to their dysfunctional ideas. If students are sneaky or evasive, you face them privately, point out the unsatisfactory behavior, and let your firm caring convey "I'm concerned about this for you." Focus on the belief they employ. Their distorted ideas may be a major life issue if they do not change them.

Many principles structuring civilized life deserve extended discussion. By enlisting your students in a search for ideas that are both true and important, you can generate much positive thought. Consider these:

What is a neighbor?
What are rights?
What is law?
What is responsibility?
What is an agreement?
What is a contract?
What is encroachment?
What is ownership?
What is a truth?
What is real?
What is good?
What is a belief?
What is justice?
What is freedom?
What is a mistake?
What is government?
What is a family?
What is integrity?
What is discipline?
What are cause and effect?
What is a model?

The idea people have about these intangibles guides how they act in society. Planting students within a reality they share with others is a solid basis for rethinking what they do. When views are opposed, you help them focus on the accurate appreciation of each: "If everyone believed this, how would it affect society?" The intent is not to convey an ideology but rather to help them make sense of what they perceive.

Rehabilitation programs in some way must confront the ideas from which offenders select reasons for their behavior and teach appropriate thinking. Any of us can remember when we had to acknowledge grudgingly that our thinking was incorrect even though our behavior continued resistant.

A clue for assisting this change in them is that behavior is driven most by the first idea that comes to our mind in a given situation, usually the one to which we have most recently given energy. So when students learn a guideline and can apply it at once in class, they are more likely to use it again later.[15]

We say, "You need to know how to do this when it's called for. To apply good thinking outside class, you need to understand how to do it first inside." Emotional satisfaction meshed with practical learning strengthens their presumption of applying it. The pleasant aura and a memory of its value in class appeal to them later.

By discussing the previous questions, we demonstrate that people examine their experience, accumulate ideas about it, and use their best thinking and that they themselves can grasp and respond to what we say. In sum, credible people embody and convey sensible ideas that students can verify from observation of reality and then apply, and for which they receive affirmation. Any of these conditions missing weakens the effort.

Structure of Thought

Although many ideas about life and society can be valuable, a scant handful typically guides a person. If we can expand their claim on specific, useful ideas, we improve the odds that they will draw on them later. Mental competence can be thought of as the range of perspectives the mind can bring to bear on an issue. Those given here comprise a tool kit for intellectual flexibility. Photocopy them for everyone, explain them, and apply them to students' experience:

1. CAUSE–EFFECT. What determines or affects what, both obvious and subtle?
2. CERTAINTY. What is absolutely certain and what uncertain?
3. COMFORT. How do people's comfort and pleasure affect their judgment?
4. COMPARE–CONTRAST. How is this the same as or different from something else?
5. EVENTS. Was this a specific happening or ongoing? Does it relate to other events past, present, or future?
6. FACT. Is this fact or opinion, an issue resolved by data or interpretation?
7. IMPORTANCE. What scale of importance should be used to judge this? What values are represented?
8. MATERIALS. What are the physical components or parts? What is seen, heard, shaped, formed, or handled?

9. MEANING. (a) What did the author say? (Quote his or her words.) (b) What did the author mean? (Use the author's other writings.) (c) What do you understand it to mean? (Draw on your own knowledge.) (d) How do you use or apply it?
10. MOTIVATION. What purpose or intent moved those who brought this about? What influences were major or minor?
11. PART–WHOLE. How is this part of something larger?
12. PATTERN. How is this ordered or patterned? How is it free, formless, or changing?
13. PEOPLE. Who is affected? Who participates? Who benefits?
14. PRINCIPLES. What are the governing ideas, the form given to major thoughts?
15. PROCESS. Is this a "how-to-do" something, a sequence of orderly activity?
16. REASONS. Is this evidence that supports something else? Does it stack up logically?
17. RULES. Is this a rule for understanding or doing something?
18. SUBJECTIVE–OBJECTIVE. Does this exist mainly in someone's mind as their view of the world or exist in external reality?
19. SUBSTANCE–QUALITY. What is the basic nature, the thing in itself? What are the characteristics of this basic nature?
20. VISIBILITY. Is this obscure, concealed, or obvious? Are appearances different from truth? Are there layers of meaning?

These factors are razors for sifting meaning. Sciences use cause–effect, part–whole, facts, and certainty. Literature draws on subjective–objective, purpose, people, principles, and qualities. Politics, government, and history are affected greatly by comfort, motivation, events, process, rules, and visibility. As you present a subject, explain how a given factor applies. Ask them to analyze their reading and assignments in terms of it, build it into the explorations you direct, and apply it to new viewpoints they encounter. Add factors you want them to apply to new situations.

Eventually students need to face the intellectual and moral effort involved in finding truth. The common offense is people priding themselves on asserting they are right instead of being pleased at grasping possible correction. A professor who had authored a set of history books was asked by a student what he had come to believe was the most difficult virtue to practice.

"Intellectual honesty," he replied. Without it, all other problems get worse. We all face an obligation to welcome correction, counteract our desire to please ourselves, and restrain our mind from bending information. You model this by modifying your own ideas with new information, and thanking them when they correct you. Only conscious effort removes distortion from our description of reality.

27. GUIDE BEHAVIOR

The secret of success is strenuous limitation, an editorial writer declared. People focus their energy as a powerhouse confines a flow of water to generate electricity. We attempt this with students, to channel cerebral exercise into a whole mind-body experience affecting their entire lives.

We can direct their behavior in the classroom, but to make it last, we break it into steps. They learn, practice, and apply the steps and gain confidence that they can do hard things on their own. Napoleon Bonaparte, asked why he drove his army so hard, replied, "If you make everything hard, then the truly hard things become easy." Only the discipline to acquire a competence supplies the competence when it is needed.

Correct Small Things

A change in police attention in New York City improved public safety by focusing on small things. Checking minor misbehaviors communicated that they matter. Getting away with vandalism, graffiti, and misdemeanors sets a climate of lawbreaking and lack of caring. If society's representatives are indifferent to negative behavior, its orbit reasonably expands as people push the limits.[16] This applies in schools. We focus their thinking and require their behavior in small things that we want them to apply more extensively later.

Teach Values by Behavior

We teach many critical social principles by redirecting actions. We say to them, "Do this and here's why." If we instruct them to treat each other kindly but ignore it when one hurts another, we contradict ourselves. If no consequence occurs at school, students are led to believe that none occurs in life. If students learn enough to graduate but their hurting others is passed over, they assume that as long as they perform the required, how they treat others does not matter. Schools may unwittingly teach that right answers are more important than an injury of another, a belief certain to bring unhappiness. Think how significant the following competences can become:

How to persist till a task is completed.
How to prioritize.
How to admit a mistake and apologize.
How to receive correction gracefully.
How to listen.
How to work out a conflict.
How to be a partner or teammate.
What to do in an emergency.
How to encourage another.

How to help others be successful.

Practice Behavioral Skills

If we want our lessons to make a difference, we have to root them in what we ask students to do, especially as we offer them templates for situations likely to occur outside our guidance. When you know what you want them to do later, explain how. Supply the accompanying perceptions and thoughts. Then do them in school while surrounding them with good feelings. Add behavioral patterns you find useful yourself, arrange for students to learn them, and provide a rationale for applying them.

28. USE CONSEQUENCES

Your love shows up in your caring concern for children and the pleasure you take in meeting their needs and making them successful. Caring is not only positive feelings. You meet needs by disciplining yourself to attend to what is best for them, overcoming any emotional variability in yourself. Character, as the saying goes, is what you do in spite of your moods. From within your self-discipline, your actions elicit their better actions.

Here we look at your actions of (1) being clear and firm, (2) using behavior instead of feelings as a signal for change, (3) causing students the minimum discomfort to redirect them, (4) exerting a continuum of impact on them, (5) applying consequences for distraction, and (6) awarding Bonus Time.

Clear and Firm

Rules are part of a system enabling students to learn alongside others. When they are clear, you can administer consequences decisively while remaining positive and barely hesitating in the lesson.[17]

Although your rules may be clear, the consequences of breaking them may not, which can help you. You want students thinking "If I misbehave, things could get a whole lot worse." In the Middle East there is a saying, "If you know the ransom of your hostage, kill him." That is, if you know the effect of your behavior and can accept it, you may do what you please. Students may estimate that a misbehavior is worth the price of a known, minimal consequence they will endure for it, so you may wish to leave open the sanction you apply.

Firm describes a boundary on their behavior, not rigidity in you. You sustain a limitation on them despite pressure against it, upholding a standard even against opposition. Many find this difficult.

"Dad, they just tear the subs apart," my son commented about his high school classes one day. Students not even in the class would stroll in, act as though they belonged, give a false name, talk as they pleased, and entertain themselves at the teacher's expense.

"Some subs come in, though, and from the minute they open their mouth, you know you can't mess with them," he continued. "They'll let you go so far and no farther." If you happen to have soft boundaries, notice whether they obtain the classroom experience you intend.

Behaviors versus Feelings as Signal

With some students, adult anger is a code. They hear, "Pay attention! Danger!" and listen intently until it passes. Because of the brief gain in their attention, you may resort to anger to manage them when clarity and firmness are enough. If you use your unhappiness as the signal that you demand a behavior change, they may wait for it before changing. Then, for you to manage the classroom, you need to spend hours a day on the edge of unhappiness. You guarantee that they will "make" you that way if that is the point when they impact you enough for you to require them to change. You set it up that way.

This is significant for their later life. They need to recognize conditions for an early rather than a late signal to change their behavior, or they may go through life wondering "Why are people always mad at me?" You want them to note how their act triggers an impersonal rule you administer while retaining good feelings yourself. Once establishing a standard that brings about a return to classroom attention, you need not feel even hesitant about applying it—even though regretfully, because you would prefer not to have to cause them discomfort.

Create Discomfort

Classroom progress depends on having students' attention. We may correct individuals to obtain it, but when that is insufficient, uncomfortable consequences are our next step. Behavior is governed by its perceived benefit or loss, which provides us a guideline:

DISCOMFORT TODAY = COOPERATION TOMORROW

Discomfort does not imply negative feelings but only a motivating condition, like wanting to remove a rock in your shoe. In the opening scene of the movie *Patton*, General George S. Patton, commander of the Third Army during the World War II invasion of Europe, speaks to the troops of his command: "Your mission is not to go and give your life for your country. Your mission is to make your enemy give his life for his country."

We might term this The Patton Principle: Cause discomfort in your students rather than allowing them to cause discomfort in you. Keep your own good feelings while administering discipline, and be unswayed by attempts to manipulate you.

But observe whether the consequences you apply bring the change you want. Sometimes they fail to touch the motives for misbehavior. Students may be glad to be sent out of class to the principal's office or remain after school because they would rather not go home anyway.

A Continuum of Impact

Arrange your options by their intensity of impact and use the minimal that works. Focus students on the lesson effectively and other issues diminish. Meet their emotional needs constructively and they are less likely to meet them destructively. Assuming you do the former, you can also draw on a hierarchy of personal impact:

Start with a look: You glance at the student. He or she meets your eye, recognizes your message, and adjusts.

A longer look communicates, "I notice what you're doing, it's unacceptable, and I'm going to keep on you till you change." It need not be a glare but just a look. The message is delivered and the student adjusts.

If the student still doesn't change, you increase the impact and so must understand the next increment in this class for this student—often approaching and facing. You bring your longer look closer, limiting the student's behavior neutrally. You calm yourself and face the student at the same eye level.

The most powerful word you can use is the student's name: "Charles." Your tone implies a positive motive. "Do you need something, perhaps?" If a car ran over his dog or his parents just announced their divorce, you would like to know. "Could we make an adjustment here?" or "Can I help you with something?"

Next in the sequence is a description of the unacceptable behavior. This is not blame, threat, nor even a request for a change, but information conveyed gently: "Jennifer, you're talking while Aaron is giving his answer," a positive message rather than a rebuke. It implies, "You may not realize the effect of your action, and just knowing it you may want to adjust."

Next, request the behavior you want. Describe it in words and tones you would be glad to have the student imitate later (your modeling, of course, works constantly): "I would appreciate it if . . . ," or "It's your turn," or "It's hard to listen to two people at the same time," or "Please follow what's on the board now."

You may need to explore motivation. Assume that their behavior poses a question and you find out what it is: "Are you trying to find a way to get things done? Get your viewpoint out? Lift your mood? Be helpful to the class? Change your feeling?" Rhythmic tapping or minor eruptions may signal energy diverging from the current task. Cynical words and attitudes may warrant a challenge: "Let me explain what we're trying to do here."

Focus on the desired behavior rather than the undesired. An unconscious mechanism responds unexpectedly to commands like "Stop making noise!" or "Stop interrupting!" or "Stop snickering!" If you often find yourself using the word Stop, it is critical that you find a new strategy. Note the form of the phrase "find a new strategy." It pictures an act different from what you were doing. You weren't "finding a new strategy" a minute ago, so here we insert a different instructional CD into your internal computer. If instead the sentence had read " . . . so stop doing that!", what imagery is left? The imagery does not change. "Doing that" is still pictured even though it has an X through it.

The unconscious mind does not easily process grammatical niceties X-ing out what we don't want, our ways to say no. It prefers direct nouns and verbs to picture. More important, when it hears "making noise," "interrupting," and "snickering," it replays them as guidelines: "That's what I'm supposed to do."

An illustration occurred years ago when Philip Morris cigarettes advertised "Less Irritation." Sales dropped nationwide, so the company asked smokers what came to mind about Philip Morris cigarettes. The answer they received was "Irritation." The word "less" and the implied comparison to other cigarettes was lost. "Irritation" remained the primary image.

Even on minor issues, be clear and brief in speaking. Notice which of you blinks first—an unconscious signal of deference. Staying "inside students' space" makes it difficult for them to dismiss you. When they realize you will not back down, they eventually adjust. Maintain eye contact silently until you receive a nod of compliance.

For more serious behavior, you have parent conferences, making a plan, suspension, time-out, in-school detention, after-school detention, a talk with the principal, time with the counselor, and finally transfer to a facility that can manage the behavior. Use the minimum that works. Extreme sanctions invite manipulation, give reason for rebellion, and incline you to relax a rule.

Consequences for Distraction Time

The value students place on freedom enables a fine-tuned but minimal consequence operating early in the spectrum of misbehavior, a one-minute loss of freedom for a one-minute distraction.

Assuming you can either hold students after class or require them to return later, even keeping them one minute immediately after the bell has an impact. Urgency escalates when they are poised to leave. Your steps are:

1. Obtain a timer with a stopwatch denominated in seconds.
2. Explain that whenever some do not respond to your request for attention, you will say, "Class!" and wait five seconds. Count "one elephant, two elephants" up to five during which they can complete their sentences, return to their seats, and face you (three checkable behaviors). Elementary classes might help you select a daily timing phrase that takes a second to repeat, such as from current events (one indictment, two indictments . . .) or from science (one Bernoulli, two Bernoullis . . .).
3. If they are not quiet in five seconds, raise the stopwatch and press it to begin. When they are attentive, press it to stop. Save the total and add to it as needed later.
4. At the end of the period or day, ask them to put their books away and sit quietly after the bell for the accumulated time. Do it with a smile: "We all need a little quiet time every day, don't we?" The discomfort of the delay is minor but enough to spur one to whisper to another, "Hey, cut it out. Time is starting." By setting aside anything that interests them, you help them savor the slow passage of time they regard as theirs after they were careless with time they considered yours.

You might note special urgency at work when headed out the door late for an appointment while juggling a briefcase, a sandwich, and a cup of coffee, and your cell phone rings with a call you have to take. Check your watch also and feel how long it takes for a minute to pass. For some students, waiting while seconds tick off is like a near-death experience. Others are just uncomfortable enough to pay better attention tomorrow.

Classes may react differently. Independent high school students facing the new consequence midyear were restive. One confided that they were discussing how to "stuff the timer down the teacher's throat" but in a class meeting worked out satisfactory modifications. Try to set it up as but one feature of a system that includes interesting learning activities and an opportunity to earn free time.

Students may object that all should not suffer for the behavior of a few. You can agree if you wish and apply consequences only to misbehavers, but it divides the class and interferes with the cohesion you want. You might say instead:

> It's too complicated for me to keep track of how much time individuals distract the class. We're all in this together. Even one person distracting affects everyone. Most of the time, you can just remind someone near you that I'm asking for attention. When I say 'Class' and others don't notice, just point it out to them.

Besides ignoring you when you ask for their attention, some may disrupt an ongoing activity. Hold up the timer silently for a few seconds as a reminder and then begin timing until the disruption ceases.

Bonus Time

For many desired behaviors, students need only a stimulus—a word from us or a classmate, applause, time appearing on the clock, completion of a particular activity, checkoff on a rating scale, score appearing, and so on. Bonus Time helps mark an equivalence between their effort and acknowledgment of it.

Discuss with students a collective benefit to work toward. They might like to watch an entertaining video, play games, have free time, do a creative project, or accumulate time to apply to a larger purpose. You might have resources available like audiovisual or sports equipment, or computers.

They accumulate time as you reward minute for minute their high-value, observable behavior such as a student doing Impromptu Performance or a group doing Perfect Conversation. At the end of a day, for example, a randomly selected student stands and is asked all the questions from the day's work. The elapsed time of his or her performed answers can earn equal time for the whole class. Or a small group carries out all the Perfect Conversation skills and you match their "perfect" talking time with reward time for the class up to any cap you place on it. For managing distractions, you can assign them a presumptive hourly bonus of five minutes, and then reduce it a minute for each minute they divert the class (and increase it as they accomplish deeds you specify).

Bonus Time can encourage them to maintain the month's learning the way players' scores benefit their team. Questions and answers are already organized and summarized in their notebooks, and answer quantities are timed (or counted) and initialed by a listener. Only this clear definition of claimed learning makes the Bonus game possible.

To create it, (1) date new questions in students' notebooks when they first learn them. (2) When you wish to play the game, draw a student's name at random. (3) They hand you their notebook and you ask the questions from the prior day's work. (4) Time the answers, and add the amount to the class reward time up to any cap you place on it. Accumulating five minutes a day, students earn a bonus period in ten days. (5) With the questions numbered and dated, you can also draw a random time period. Drop tokens into a bag labeled Yesterday, Five Days, Ten Days, Twenty Days, and Thirty Days (i.e., the same day of the week for the past several weeks). Draw a token, count back that number of school days on the calendar, find the questions from that date in the student's notes, and ask them (using the following days' questions if needed to fill out the time). (6) Use up the reward time when convenient.

29. COUNSELOR CORNER

Specific students may present challenges despite constructive group activities. A few tools used together may affect their behavior quickly, based on the principle that students gladly respond to accurate, objective feedback they help generate. Little time may be needed. Once a direction is agreed on, followups may take only a few minutes for the self-checks that sustain their interest.

The Narrative

Their concept about their life is a sound starting point. All need a constructive long-term view they can draw on to guide their current behavior. The sample here can be elaborated according to the need. Sentences are presented with the conviction of fact rather than as an opinion of the counselor:

> You are growing, inevitably. You will continue to replace strategies and feelings you learned earlier with better ones to apply now. You will become independent of adults and learn how to live your own life. Like a tomato plant, you draw in resources from what surrounds you. A plant takes in nutrients—light, water—and uses them continually to reconstruct itself. Besides the physical elements your body needs, you also do the same with new ideas. School is a set of resources for you to use now. You are certain to encounter others later.

Note that the narrative is entirely free of conflict, failure, stress, or obligation. Efforts to change have a different place (see below). The narrative is instead a description of ongoing reality, pictured as the mind naturally absorbing good ideas from its surroundings, poor ideas changing gradually to better ones, and growth manifesting in greater competence and mastery of life. If they don't have this picture yet, they need to hear it from the counselor.

Presence of Feelings

Students often find it difficult to explain what they feel, even though it may influence them powerfully. To tap this zone, place in front of them the list of feelings in Appendix 1. Say, "Draw a circle around each feeling you've felt in the last couple weeks."

Students typically circle some positive and some negative. As you wish, you can elicit the story or experience behind each. To open subsequent meetings, ask, "Please put a 'b' beside any feeling getting better, and 'w' beside any getting worse." Inquire "What caused the change?" When feelings improve, ask what enabled this to occur, eliciting their strategy for managing feelings.

Their strategy has two elements, one entirely inward. If a negative feeling persists, ask them to assign it an intensity on a scale of 1–10. Then see if they can reduce the intensity by just a single number solely by inner means. Nearly everyone can do this, illustrating that they have a direct capacity to guide or steer the feeling. They are not helpless before it. Uncover changes due to their direct ability to influence a feeling.

The second element manages outer circumstances. Can they avoid settings or interactions likely to make matters worse? What do they do in those situations?

Progress Ladder

Most students are so immersed in their present life that they fail to recognize how their behavior now affects their life later. The Progress Ladder helps them understand.

Enlarge and duplicate Appendix 8 so it fills a sheet of paper for easy reading. Place it in front of them, and ask them to read it carefully. Then in the first empty column to the right of the text, place a dot showing their estimate of where they themselves stand on the scale, and underline or star the sentences that "stood out for them," the reasons they placed themselves at that point and the issues they need to work on.

For many students, the self-check arouses new motivation. You can talk out the implication of sentences they selected. They can write a paragraph describing the change they wish to make and set a daily time to read it. When you meet next, return to the Progress Ladder and have them place a new dot in the next column to the right. Connect up their self-ratings to form a line chart. As they work up the ladder, have them continue identifying the sentences marking their next step.

What Goes on Inside Them?

Ask them to write out their answers to five questions for you: (1) What am I good at? (2) What gives me joy now or when I was younger? (3) What things made me who I am? (4) What do others see in me? (5) What decisions have I made about myself?

The first four answers (listed even telegraphically) often provide clues to their life and an opening to correct misapprehensions. School staff may notice strengths and resources students are unaware of. The most significant question is usually the last one. By means of their decisions they cope with their fears, self-limitations, life view, conflicts, values, and resolutions, typically opening many avenues for followup.

Social Relations

Many students are unhappy with peers but blind to how they generate distance. They appreciate knowing easy actions that quickly improve their relationships. Duplicate Appendix 9 or create a simpler one that fits your students' needs. Design it so they can rate themselves objectively and insert a number for each skill in the appropriate space.

The activity of doing the rating is more important than the number they write in. To assess themselves, they hold a criterion in mind and match it against their actions. Merely doing this several times teaches a connection: This skill applies to this situation. Their awareness of choosing a response is your first objective and leads naturally to steps of improvement. You can discuss their experiences with a skill at any depth they comprehend (cf. 11), but such discussions matter more as students immediately connect them to a self-rating.

Thought-Changing

Inappropriate behavior follows from a thought applied in that situation (cf. 24 for more details). Find out "What were you thinking about that? What goes through your head as X happens?" Make guesses about it until the student says, "Yeah, that's it." Write down their thought verbatim, and then pose a challenge: "That thought doesn't work very well, does it? Could you and I work out a better one?" Collaboratively, write out an antidote-thought of a sentence or two, and ask "Could you 'go to' that one instead of the other when the experience comes up again?"

Resolve any reservations. Even a single detrimental thought switched to a constructive form can spark a major turnabout. In followup meetings, students often like to relate how their new thought "worked," while others prefer to write a "b" (better) or "w" (worse) beside it. Explore edits that could improve it.

What Is Going to Happen?

School people are often mystified at students' inability to realize that their actions have consequences. If they do not get this material learned, if they do not get this assignment in, if they do not show up in class—they won't pass the course. If they fail the course, they will not graduate, and so on. How could this not be clear?

An unexpected finding explains. When students are asked to imagine themselves in the future, an area of the brain associated with other people lights up instead of the area associated with themselves. They essentially think, "Someone else is going to handle this later."[18] To stretch their identification with their own actions—consequences and all—use Mental Movie (cf. 8). Plant them inside noticing "This is me" with their sense of self intact, and then move it incrementally into the future.[19]

30. ATTENTION DEFICITS

Distractibility poses a challenge for some students. A way to think about it is that they need to learn consciously to do what others do automatically.

When a student says, "I have ADHD," you are not obliged to say, "Oh you poor thing. I guess you'll have a hard life." Instead ask, "What do you enjoy doing?" They will name a sport, a personal interest, or a video game—activities dependent on sustained attention. When you then inquire, "How do you manage to continue paying attention to it?", they have no answer because they do not understand how their preferred activity and their schoolwork differ.

Point out that with the former, they learned what constituted distractions and decided not to respond to them. They identify a presence in their awareness and make a choice about it—internal efforts that counteract distractions. The same choice applied in school has a huge impact on their learning. Many never learned how to manage their attention and may make rapid changes once they understand. Pursue several threads:

Sustain an Interesting Thought

Find out what they enjoy doing, such as a game, and help them notice how easily they sustain thought about it. Explain how they comparably can sustain a train of thought about a school subject. Check back on their progress at this. They say to themselves, "I choose to return to this focus."

Handle Stop-and-Start Better

Acknowledge to them that instruction constantly interrupts and redirects their attention, making it harder to continue any thought that interests them. Many moments ask them to renew their intention: "Now, I focus on this." The compartments of their life inevitably require them to do this by choice.

Assess Environmental Factors

Their performance may vary under conditions such as proximity to others, background sounds, and external interruptions. Some work better with headphones, others by adding music. With homework, help them figure out the optimal study setting for their home conditions and notice classroom circumstances you can alter to reduce distraction.

Rate Concentration Units

Explain to them how to calculate their concentration units (CUs) (cf. 36), and at first ask them to do this hour by hour. They bring you their numerical scores, and together you plot them on a line chart.

Rate Sustained Focus

Print out a blank chart (Appendix 6), use ordinary graph paper, or create your own. Lay it landscape and make the bottom line 0 and the top 100. Start with a mark in the middle:

> Let's assume right now your level of sustained focus is average. You and I are talking like you usually do. Each hour from now through the school day, go to the next vertical line and make another mark on that line reflecting how well you kept your mind on what you were doing, okay?

Reflecting on their score ties their behavior to the attention that takes control of it. They are also nudged to improve because they like to see any line rise that represents their progress.

Chapter Five

Practice Learning

To adapt "practice makes permanent" to the classroom, we examine what comprises the practice of knowledge and makes it effective (cf. 5. Partner Practice). We note how to apply it to numbers; with knowledge of varying exactness, with small amounts of time, and for beginning students; in conversation outside school; and with methods that lead to perfect recall.

31. PEG LIST

The natural way to forestall forgetting is to wait a moment and recall. A few glances at a fresh impression are often sufficient to hold it. Running errands, we meet a family friend, converse a bit, and easily remember it and tell others at home. Thinking about it even briefly sustains our memory.

Schools, instead of providing the later glances to maintain ideas, constantly override them. We load students' wheelbarrow, make them dump it, and load it again. With most of what we present, they must start over even to begin installing it, wasting the first imprint we made in their short-term memory.

One day I discovered an easy alternative. After concentrating for a couple hours, I needed a change of pace. Thinking just to use my mind differently, I went to my shelf and picked out a book on Roman history, cracked it at random, and found myself immersed in the Roman civil war. Sulla's army raced to defend Rome from opposing forces and defeated them. Sulla then ordered his troops to butcher his captured foes in earshot of his conference with the Senate.

After reading a page, I felt a shift in my attention, returned to my desk, set a timer for five minutes, and resumed my work. After what seemed but a moment, the timer went off. I stopped what I was doing, turned my mind back to Rome, and without reviewing the pages, could remember the scenes vividly. Later I did the same with a page from a book on organizational development. Again five minutes later, the knowledge remained. On a slip of paper on my desk, I noted "Sulla" and "organize/problem solving." Following days added other words about current events, personal incidents, research, and reading. A brief daily mental review of the list, often just while driving, was enough to retain their substance. The list gradually became an ongoing index of everything I wanted to save for active thought, a way to peg interesting ideas I had run across. See what you draw from this list:

attention deficit
choice to focus
self-rating
Peg List
Sulla
wait, recall

Perhaps you recall what the words refer to from the prior section and preceding paragraphs or easily recover their meaning with a glance. You focus attention on the terms only long enough to restore their main meaning.

Such brief but focused time in input/output can enable students to save enormous knowledge with little effort. You might identify the points yourself or leave their selection to students: "We have fifteen minutes left in the period. Please read your history book for items for your Peg List."

A student may note six ideas during math and then begin social studies. He takes a few seconds during the latter to recheck the images from math. By the end of the day, he has reaffirmed the ideas on his list a dozen times, sinking them deeply into memory with no time taken from other obligations. To track an idea to a reference, students can note a page number with the peg.

32. THE PRACTICE ELEMENT

The practice element is the degree to which students draw on a previously absorbed internal model of their knowledge. Peg List is one way to do it and tests are a common example. To practice, students supply knowledge from their own store of it. Preparing for a test, their practice is drawing knowledge out of themselves. The more pieces they already have inside, the more they can express. We distinguish three levels.

Low

In activities with a low practice element, students are passive, needing no prior internal model. Knowledge comes to them from outside their own mind. A teacher may lecture while they take notes. They may read, watch videos or movies, listen to audiotapes or to other students answering questions, or ask questions of the teacher. Silent seat work may focus them on recognition, matching, linking, filling in blanks, or copying.

They carry out these activities with little attention and do not depend on knowledge already mastered. Done alone, these activities do not install knowledge but may compile a model of the knowledge that later effort deepens.

Medium

With medium practice element, some knowledge begins outside the student and some inside, but the student does call up an internal model to develop further.

Students can help each other correct errors, prioritize ideas, select the most important aspects to work on, offer analogies and ways to remember, convert information to questions and answers, summarize in writing, reorganize notes, have experiences and do experiments, and analyze with a new viewpoint something already learned.

Writing helps to solidify the inner form of the knowledge at this level and to confirm meanings that otherwise remain vague. Students learn steadily as they spend time in the medium practice element.

High

Here the student already possesses all the pieces of knowledge used. Drawing on them reinforces their inner model most fully. Students answer questions, explain their knowledge to a listener without help, debate issues about the subject, take tests, write without using prior notes, do any medium practice element with material drawn entirely from memory, or employ methods from our design like Impromptu Performance, Mental Movie, Walk Away, and Time Capsule. To make learning both rapid and permanent, arrange for them to work as long as possible in high practice element activities. To save anything, ask them to output answers until they are mastered.

Larson's design for increasing college students' learning applied the latter two levels and should be suitable for senior high. Students paired up and studied two pages of text at a time. Then without looking at notes or diagrams, the recaller summarized the pages as completely as possible. The listener corrected errors and misunderstandings, noted omissions, and helped create novel ways of recalling the information. Recaller and listener switched roles every two pages and worked steadily through a part in one sitting. They clarified what they learned from each other and how they could improve their use of time and helped each other by judging importance, elaborating on each other's summaries with images and analogies, and personalizing the material. Efforts at summarizing improved retention.[20]

33. DESIGNATED LISTENER

An anxious, awkward, ill-dressed little girl from a large family lived at the end of a rural school bus route driven by a warm and friendly woman. Every day going and coming, the two had a few minutes of private time to talk. When the girl graduated after twelve years, confident and competent, she told the driver with great feeling that their few minutes of daily conversation were the difference enabling her to "make it."

Everyone deserves someone who will listen to them daily and unfailingly. An attentive, outside-the-classroom listener is so encouraging that it pays rich dividends to make sure each student has someone. In class, students listen to each other to practice their learning, but a different impact occurs when a person outside the classroom waits eagerly to hear their new knowledge.

Parents are the first choice, but if they cannot, look for a sibling, older student, senior citizen, relative, or school employee whose interest in children is not exhausted by their job. Ask Designated Listeners to commit reliably to a time of day when they can take five to ten minutes. A few qualities make this work:

1. The listener offers only attention and interest, not urging, suggesting, changing anything, or guiding—unless the student invites this. For the experience to work, the atmosphere needs to be entirely free of pressure.
2. The beginning content is "Tell me everything you learned today"—both academic and social. The question makes sense only if the design of instruction produces conscious, mastered knowledge hour by hour. Trying to explain only the familiarized, superficial knowledge emerging from most classrooms is inevitably frustrating. Students grasp pieces here and there but cannot integrate them. Their experience of explaining courts failure constantly. Listeners might also ask questions from previous material, find out what the student considers important or interesting, and concentrate always on what he or she can already talk about successfully. Students, of course, can bring up anything they want to say.

3. To help Designated Listeners, you can compile guidelines, suggest communication skills from the CSCS (Appendix 9), make up a check-off calendar they can post on their refrigerator, or send home the factors for Perfect Conversation, the questions for exploring a topic (cf. 14), and the perspectives for understanding (cf. 26) for older students.
4. Designated Listeners might also wish to meet occasionally to discuss how to make their few minutes fruitful, support the class in other ways, and help each other with the challenges of their children's education.
5. Two qualities making this activity welcome to both parents and students are the limited commitment of time and the focus on success. The hard work of installing the knowledge has been done at school and now comes the easy part, increasing its value to students and integrating it into their thinking.

34. PRIMARY GRADES

Most of the methods here adapt readily to primary grades. The steps are not complicated, signals of effort are evident, rewards come quickly, emotional needs are met, and simple criteria assure them that they meet expectations.

For presenting knowledge, two points of access are their imagination and talkativeness. Experiences, hands-on activity, stories, posters, and pictures impress images into their heads. The output for them is to tell the story of their learning: Tell how they care for the guinea pig; tell about the seasons; tell how to make bread; tell about the calendar; tell the story of Arnold's adventure; tell about The Little Engine That Could; tell about any historical event or person; tell what they learned on the field trip; tell about colors, letters, words, and numbers; tell about the world. Their performance is to tell their story to a listening partner.

If the notion of one kindergartner listening attentively to another challenges credulity, note that the behavior comprises a scant few concrete details easily conveyed: (1) Keep your mouth shut, (2) look at the other student, and (3) wait till they are done. We can drill such guidelines until they master them. With them we can process an enormous amount of knowledge.

A means of doing this is to give them a simple instruction they repeat out loud together and then perform in pairs.

Practice Format

Stand them in two rows facing each other. In their own row, they are side by side with others, looking toward their partner who stands in a parallel row a couple of feet away. One row might place their toes on a strip of red paper: "You're the Reds." The others toe a green strip: "You're the Greens." Teach any two things this way with pictures on the floor: whales and elephants, crickets and beetles, ships and planes. Ask them all to point to their partner opposite and make sure pairs find each other. Then practice the microsteps one at a time:

> "Reds, raise your hands." They do. They know who they are.
>
> "Reds, I want you to ask a question of the Greens. Now what are you going to do?"
>
> They answer in chorus, "Ask a question of the Greens!"
>
> You say again, "Reds, I want you to ask a question of the Greens. Now what are you going to do?"
>
> Again they answer and stragglers chime in, "Ask a question of the Greens."
>
> "Greens, I want you to answer the question. Now, what will you do?"
>
> They shout together, "Answer the question!"
>
> Then, "Reds, after you ask the question of your partner, you'll listen to their answer. Now, what will you do after you ask the question?" They respond, "Listen to the answer!" Do the same thing with the Greens.

Get them to repeat the directions in increments as small as needed until everyone has them cold. Then feed them content one question at a time for which you have supplied the answer, starting with the familiar for guaranteed success:

"When I tell you the question, I want you to say it to your partner right after me. So Reds, the first question to ask your partner is, 'What is your name?'" They do so in a babble of voices. You ask them to switch roles with the same question and proceed to whatever you want to teach.

Clear Maps

You install a clear map. You guarantee everyone's success piece by piece by telling questioners the sentence to ask (they repeat it after you till all have it) and telling answerers what to answer (they repeat it after you till all have it). Then you direct them to do it on their own with their partner. With this basic sequence, address any content. When everyone has mastered school rules and classroom guidelines, proceed into points of knowledge.

At times they help each other make sure "all the steps are in the right order" or "all the parts are there." You may wish to score their collective ability to tell back their knowledge and compile the class's growing number of points of knowledge on a wall chart while assuring everyone 100% success. All are encouraged that they measure up to expectations perfectly.

Our own actions must be clear. Children wonder, "What do I do first? What do I do next?" We resolve their confusion with a multistep map: They (1) line up, (2) identify a partner, (3) get the question straight, (4) identify the source of the answer such as on a wall chart or in a book or in your ringing words, (5) ask the question, (6) give the answer, and (7) trade roles. When they learn that answer, they (8) identify the next thing to learn.

They can use these steps to learn anything, and their reciprocity and energy seem like a game they always win at. Drill the map of the action steps, run it for a few days, and they have it perfectly. The less clear it is, the more likely they will back off. If they have learned to fear mistakes, they think, "I'm not going to try this seriously until I know I won't embarrass myself." Once they know they can do it successfully, it becomes your permanent, cost-free ally.

Memory Bank

Students can master and claim their learning with these three steps:

1. On an index card, they write a question on the front and its answer on the back, and collect their cards in a personal box, bag, or cup labeled Memory Bank.
2. They practice each card until they can tell it without looking at it that day and consider it mastered when they can do this on three separate days, which they note on the card.
3. They make up a duplicate card to take home and present to their parents. Parents are encouraged to ask them the question, listen to the answer, celebrate their competence, and deposit the duplicate in a home Memory Bank kept on the kitchen table or other prominent place for ongoing practice.

35. MEMORY HOOKS

The basic memory aid is the intrinsic structure of a subject illuminating how everything relates to everything else.

Structuring

Many students benefit from parts fitting together into logical structures. Students might master a subject by spending the first few days learning the text's table of contents. Talk through it to help them understand how parts and chapters fit the whole. If a text has five parts, for instance, why are there five parts? The relations between them offer fundamental understanding about the subject. Use the Time Capsule method or Content Scoreboard chunk by chunk to retain the table of contents perfectly (cf. 38 and 47).

Then when you proceed through the text in detail, every new idea already finds a logical niche in a prior structure ever more deeply understood and reinforced, basic knowledge constantly affirmed and developed as a natural scaffold for everything else. Students both remember and comprehend.

Artificial aids run the risk of removing focus from the subject. Students may later recall the hooks perfectly without connecting them to the knowledge, though some can be useful.

Number Code

A number code links the sound of certain letters to specific numbers.

Use it to compose a phrase easy to remember that offers a clue to the meaning and sequence of the numbers. A common code is 1 = the letter T (think of the single downstroke of the letter); 2 = the letter N (two downstrokes), 3 = M (three downstrokes), 4 = R (rr sound in four), 5 = L (Roman numeral for 50), 6 = CH, SH, J (the chuh, shuh, juh sound), 7 = hard K sound (both sounds in "cake"), 8 = F (think of the double loop of the cursive f), 9 = B, P (letters b and p are both inversions of 9), and 0 = S, Z, and soft C (as in "zero" and "city").

Using just the first consonant of a word to represent its number, students can translate number sequences into a hint of their meaning. The first five digits of pi might translate clumsily as "Move Turns Round to Join," the initial consonants indicating 3.1416. Columbus happening upon America in 1492 becomes "Traveling aRmada Pinta Nina," again using the first consonant in each word. Class creativity can convert formulas, mathematical relationships, and dates into phrases all can learn easily.

Loci Method

A framework for remembering a sequence of ideas is to select a visual analogy for a given point of knowledge and join it to a naturally occurring sequence you can picture easily.

Once I gained almost total recall of a difficult course by placing it all on two streets I was familiar with near my home. I would identify a point I wanted to remember, invent a visual analogy for it, locate it beside a house I knew well, and work my way around the house, placing the analogical forms near windows, corners, fences, and yard characteristics, and then move on to the next house. To indicate an ascending sequence I used a ladder propped beside a door; for a reference to a part and whole, a large pie with pieces cut; a concept contained within another was a small can nested inside a larger one, and so on.

An unexpected benefit was that representing concepts visually required me to understand them, so that I found myself readily integrating them later. A similar technique worked well for remembering the substance of a lecture. I chose a familiar room, assigned visual symbols to the points of the lecture, and placed them clockwise around the room. This helped me understand them, recall their substance, and make time pass quickly.

Represent Knowledge

Individuals hold onto knowledge by different handles, mainly seeing (visual), hearing/saying (auditory), and feeling/doing (kinesthetic). Regardless of the aspects of intelligence in which students may be strong or weak, we need to enable everyone to bridge into a common fund of shared knowledge. To achieve this overlap, (1) we use multiple forms of representation in presenting knowledge, and (2) students bridge from one form to another in expressing it. Whatever the form of input the student prefers, the output phase can include the others.

An all-purpose vehicle incorporating the three forms of representation is for teachers to describe in words the abstractions, pictures, diagrams, and structural forms presented visually, and for students to write, explain, and perform them. A student who relies mainly on hearing words picks up sounds and then puts visuals to them. One who appreciates the pictures and diagrams listens also for the words and then speaks them. One who best writes them listens, watches, and speaks. They receive knowledge as they best do so, translate it inwardly to the other forms needed, and output the expanded knowledge.

Students who appear to gather much from presentation and discussion and little from reading may be predominantly auditory. An acquaintance of the author was a doctor who graduated medical school without taking notes, to the consternation of his teachers. He sat in the front row and simply remembered everything spoken. If you suspect such a bent in a student, inquire:

"Would you rather 'Play the tape' or 'See the movie' for remembering what we've discussed?"
"Does this come through your mind word by word?"
"Do you sometimes recall what people say verbatim?"
"Do you get more from my explanations or from reading by yourself?"

If they are predominantly auditory, suggest that they "replay what I just said" instead of picturing it.

For the visually oriented, many textbooks have an eye-catching array of illustrations. Ask them to scan the pictures in their text and employ a visual memory method such as Mental Movie (cf. 8).

Diagrams

Students may possess unique skills to draw on. An artistic and intelligent boy complained that he could not remember ideas the way others did. Asked to convert each key point into a visual and link together the day's assignment creatively, he was able to do this almost as fast as he could write and had the material learned in few minutes.

Make it a class project to develop interesting ways to assimilate knowledge. They might invent diagrams, association of images, time lines, causal relationships, visual or logical structures, and imaginative links. Ask them to outline what they want to remember and then together devise the easiest way for everyone to grasp it.

Kinesthetics

Those who represent knowledge through physical sensations benefit especially from writing out lecture notes and summaries. Invite them to draw outlines, maps, and symbolic representations. Physical movement may aid their effort to represent qualities hard to put into words. The Total Physical Response method succeeds in teaching foreign languages by drawing on how intimately we enlist our physical system as we manifest meaning in language.[21]

Writing

Ask everyone to create a synthesis of the notes they accumulate from your presentations and their reading. They write out a summary and place it with the answers in their notebooks. Reorganizing and summarizing is one of the fastest ways to gain in-depth understanding and ensures that the material can safely be laid aside for a longer time and with brief review be restored completely.

36. CONCENTRATION UNITS

The gain from any class activity increases as students concentrate on it. They (1) choose a focus or goal, (2) identify the effort that reaches it, (3) keep their attention on it, and (4) ignore distractions. Even subjective measurement of a skill can encourage its development.

Two scores form a CU. One is their concentration as a percentage of it as perfect. At the top, no threat or distraction diverts them from their work. At the bottom they are vulnerable to the slightest influence. A student at 10% barely pays attention, at 30% perhaps studies with a girl friend sitting nearby, and at 60% substantially follows a teacher's presentation though with mind wandering.

The second measure is the amount of time they spend at that level. Combining the ratings, we obtain CUs by multiplying the integers of the percent of concentration times the number of minutes it persists: 50% concentration for a 50-minute period = 2,500 CUs. The most gain comes not from a small change in their number of minutes in class but from a large change in concentration. A distracted class operating at 10% concentration for 50 minutes achieves 10 × 50 or 500 CUs per student. A more focused class with a 50% concentration level for 45 minutes achieves 45 × 50 or 2250 CUs. Raising their concentration to 80% even while reducing time to 40 minutes still increases CUs to 3200. Measuring CUs is way of reminding them of the impact of their degree of focus.

Invite them to estimate their concentration for the current hour and turn in their results to you. Post their scores until the next time you ask the same question and then insert the new numbers. Students asked to rate themselves usually do so close to what a teacher observes. For occasional variety, have them draw another student's name randomly. Without naming the person they observe, at the end of the class they turn in a rating for both themselves and the other student. You post each one's average of the two scores by self and other.

Resolving subtle issues can increase concentration. A high school math teacher who spent the first ten minutes of every class talking about feelings said she always got more done with the remaining time than when she tried to spend the entire period on math. Surging emotions divert attention as much as does a bulldozer outside the window.

37. WALK AWAY

How long should students spend at what activity in order to enhance long-term retention?

A study decades old answered this. Among common classroom activities such as reading, writing, lecturing, note taking, and styles of study, the best of these could revolutionize educational outcomes. The most efficient use of time found was spending 40% to 80% of it in the effort to recall. We apply such effort when we explain learning to someone else or take a test.[22]

The Walk Away method applies this idea. (1) We install a piece in our memory, (2) recall it at intervals, (3) increase the size of the pieces, and (4) increase the length of the interval between rehearsals of it. Used better for personal study at home rather than in a classroom, with twenty minutes daily students can master course notes or poetry, or in a concentrated weekend absorb a semester's notes.

Try it yourself to appreciate its pacing. First, select the material you want to learn, such as passages in a text or notes. Open them on a table. Instead of sitting as usual, stand in front of the material. This conveys to your mind that a different kind of disciplined attention will occur and also enable you to move about. You might lean over the material and look down at it with your hands planted on the table on either side of it. Being slightly uncomfortable reminds you not to relax because you will move on in a moment.

Read for two to four minutes, more briefly if the material is dense and fact-filled, and longer for the more general. Try to fix in your mind the concepts you want to save and the key words and phrases that express them. Limit yourself to three to five points at a time, working within the precision level and chunk size that fit your study goals (cf. 40. Degrees of Precision).

After you read and select the points, scan them for twenty to thirty seconds to fix them in mind. Put words to this: "Okay, there's this, point one (summarize it), and now . . . ah, here's point two (say inwardly the words that describe it). I'll include also this, point three (say it) and here's point four (say it). That's enough." Putting words to the focus of your attention makes it more definite.[23]

Straighten up, walk to the other side of the room, and aloud tell back all you can remember of what you read. This shows exactly what you know. Doing it this way alters your intent. While we read, we seldom think to ask "Do I know this or not?" Ideas flow along like a highway under our automobile. We point ourselves where we are headed rather than where we have been. This method instead causes us to look backward. Saying the words aloud makes clear just how much of where we have been still lodges in us.

When you have exhausted your memory and paused long enough to extract final bits, walk back to the material on the table. Look at it again and identify the portions remembered and those not. If you recalled points two and four and missed one and three, fix the missing pieces where they belong, and repeat. Walk away and recall everything with all the pieces included. Continue these steps—rereading, refixing the material in mind, and walking away to recount them—until you have that chunk learned. Go to another chunk, do the same with it, and combine the two, telling back everything in them.

Its unique features enhance the method. Standing during it signals an active experience replacing physical positions unconsciously associated with leisure. Walking away signals the memory that you will not rescue it from the effort to recall, and prevents you from gathering hints by quick glances at the material. You tell your mind to produce everything, which is the criterion memory activity. Saying the words aloud (or whispered if others are nearby) separates exactly what you know from what you do not. Studying wordlessly often leaves us believing we know something that we actually grasp vaguely.

38. TIME CAPSULE

Here capsules of key knowledge are retained over time. The method is easy, generates vivid, permanent memory, and especially fits subjects requiring precise recall such as foreign languages, mathematics, and science (cf. 40. Degrees of Precision).

I asked my son, age fifteen at the time, if he would try out my design.

"Six minutes a day max, total time spent," I said.

"No problem," he reported. "So what do you want me to learn?" The end of school was three weeks off. I was curious what he would choose, so I was generously vague.

"Pick anything you like, anything you would want to talk to someone about, anything you want to have as permanent learning." He drew material for five days learning from articles about rock groups and drum technique.

We applied the method described here (without boxing the capsules). He recalled the information at the intervals specified, with the total time spent in all of the recalls together around six minutes a day. As expected, he remembered perfectly everything he installed in the two minutes of study we allotted daily for his initial reading.

"Do you think you might want to use this method with some of your subjects?" I asked him casually at the end of the week.

"Yeah," he answered. "Maybe when we start studying for finals." In eleven days his school would be out. Before that, his teachers would pass a few pieces of the semester's work through students' minds one last time and then test the pieces. I sighed.

Years later I mentioned to him that I was writing about his experience.

"Funny thing is, Dad, I still remember that stuff!" he said. If his teachers had wanted to install anything from their courses permanently, they could have asked students to obtain a clear initial impression of the knowledge and then expand the interval between recalls of it. The method picks up when the students have already learned the material well enough to pass a test on it. At that point, temporary knowledge can be made permanent.

Forming Capsules

Capsuling knowledge makes absolutely clear to the mind what is worth the added effort and casts it in a form easy to practice. We express the learning in concise phrases, write them compactly, and draw a border around them.

Maybe in preparing for a college exam you distilled a course into two pages of key notes. We do the same here, except use the whole semester. From whatever you explain, you boil it down to specify the points deserving perfect recall, the key material that might show up on a comprehensive test. A high school science teacher decided that her students should learn permanently the eight signs of cancer, made a capsule of them, and everyone learned them in one period. Material goes into a capsule so you can focus on it in exactly that form.

You might designate a subject and let students choose details: "Read pages 85 to 90 in social studies and form capsules for ideas you pick out" or "Work on all the Spanish vocabulary you can for the remainder of the hour." Pages just for capsules can be added to the Answers section of their notebooks as an efficient summary of what they know, with matching questions on their Questions pages.

Capsule Size

Capsules are small so students can grasp and assimilate them readily, but too little in them offers insufficient challenge while too much overtaxes the memory. The denser the material is, such as a math formula, the smaller the capsule should be and the shorter its initial reading time. One already knows the meaning of each number, symbol, or word used and the process involved, such as to multiply or divide. All that is left is retaining it.

With an optimum size capsule, students can read it once slowly and thoughtfully, look up, be slightly challenged by it, but repeat it accurately. If they cannot quite do so, they read it one more time and again try to repeat it. If they still cannot, the capsule is too big. Reduce it by a fifth or a quarter and try again.

Weigh the information contained in both points and bits. These challenge the mind differently. Points are the part you don't know, the piece of knowledge you want to add. Four or five of these in one capsule work well and are expressed by words, symbols, or numbers you already know. These latter are the bits, each adding an essential note of meaning. Because they may be few or many, they present a somewhat separate challenge. A single new point explained by a complete paragraph of familiar bits (words) may be unwieldy.

Selecting the bits that express a point efficiently is a valuable cognitive task. In some subjects, omitting a few might leave an acceptable vagueness but not in others. Best results seem to occur with capsules of between ten and twenty bits of total information (words and numbers) but no more than seven new points. For example, five Spanish words and their English translations comprise five points with ten bits that might be arranged in parallel lists or in one to three phrases or sentences.

A capsule with four forms of the Spanish verb "to talk" would have: *hablar*—to talk, *hablo*—I talk, *hablas*—you (familiar) talk, *habla*—he/she talks. Four of these bits, the points to learn, are the Spanish verb forms. The other ten bits are English words translating them.

A capsule about Columbus might read: King Ferdinand and Queen Isabella of Portugal sent Christopher Columbus with three ships, the Pinta, Niña, and Santa Maria in 1492. Here are twenty bits conveying seven points—three names of people, three boats, and a date.

Preparing Capsules

Do this the day before installing them if you can. The mind does much of its work spontaneously overnight if fed information and an expectation.[24] Being told "Tomorrow you're going to master this perfectly," their minds attack it today. Before opening their notebooks the next day, they ask themselves "What are we installing today?" Recalling the basic subject matter and an impression of the prepared capsules, half their work is done, assuring them rapid success. The material, again, is already presented, understood, prioritized, boundaried, and arranged. All that remains is permanent retention.

When everyone understands the format, you can ask each student to design a capsule for the class from a page you assign them personally. When all are ready, they present their capsule to the group, discuss each, improve it as needed, and copy them all into their notebooks.

While students install capsules in one subject, during the expanding time intervals they can prepare capsules in another—turning their mind completely away from the material being deepened. During the designated intervals, they cleanly leave from and return to the capsuled knowledge. They might master science while reading history between recalls or master math capsules while working on language arts. If you have them for only one subject, at least direct them to nonoverlapping work. Capsule preparation is a good day-end activity for small groups, can occupy scattered pockets of time, and makes the next day more productive.

Steps to Install

Try the method yourself. Read over a capsule you have prepared and understand the information in it. Your goal is to transfer that exact external representation into a stable mental form, a 100% accurate, complete, internal version with all points and bits in place, general ideas and details.

Read it, lay it down, look away, visualize it and immediately repeat in words everything you can remember. Saying everything in words, telling all the bits at least whispered to yourself is the only way to determine for sure what you know. If you cannot put words to it immediately, you do not have exact knowledge. Describe visual elements. In a formula, put all the symbols, numbers, and steps in their right places. For lists, describe the placement of ideas—first, second, and third.

Once you can do this—read, look up, and tell the whole thing—you have an initial impression. Compare it to hammering a nail. The first tap gets it in the correct position but secured superficially, only lightly embedded in memory. The next taps drive it in solidly but depend absolutely on the first one done well.

Set a timer to beep one minute later, long enough to challenge your memory. For sixty seconds, turn your attention to something else, specifically not thinking about your first impression. Unless you do this, you do not tax your memory to hold onto it. If the capsule remains visible on your desk or included in something you scan, your mind does not mount an effort to remember. If you use a clock with a sweep second hand, either ask someone to call time at the end of each interval or do it yourself.

When the timer sounds, do the recall but do not look back at the material. The benefit to your memory arises from taxing it rather than supplying it with another surface impression. Recall everything you can from it. Only after you have tried your best and cannot remember it all, go back and study briefly any part you forgot. Look at the capsule, again recall it instantly, and repeat the one-minute interval until you can tell it back perfectly without hesitating or rechecking.

Complete recall usually occurs on the first try because you already know the material well and the interval is short. This one-minute stage is significant, however, because from there the avenue to permanent memory is clear: just increase the interval.

Set the timer for five minutes later and engage your attention elsewhere. When the timer beeps, repeat what you did after one minute. Recall the capsule completely without checking or reviewing. Do not return to the printed version unless details have dropped from memory. Repeat absolutely everything in words and include any details you missed before. If you cannot, reread it to fill in the missing pieces and repeat the same step, or return to the prior interval of one minute. Three, four, or five minutes for the second interval seem equally comparable for continuing the cycle.

Expand Intervals

The next intervals are fifteen minutes, forty-five to sixty minutes, several hours or at day's end, and preferably for two days following. Then include capsules in students' long-range mastery review to be recalled occasionally. When students are successful at the fifteen-minute time, they have an impression deep enough to be easily refreshed and practiced later.

Group Collaboration

Students enjoy the challenge of installing three capsules during one period. A different student times each one, starts off its intervals, and calls time when they are completed. Everyone begins their recall together for each capsule at the immediate and one-minute phases till all are successful. Then while the first is in its five-minute interval, a second is introduced that does not have overlapping content. With two in progress (one in its five-minute interval and the other in its fifteen-minute interval), a third can be initiated. Between recalls, the group can prepare capsules on new material and share and copy them.

When two capsules complete an interval at about the same time, they are always of different length. Each timer tells the interval for their capsule, and everyone recalls the shortest first since it is the most tenuous. The longer the interval, the deeper the capsule is already embedded and better able to sustain a delay. So if capsules with five-, fifteen-, and forty-five-minute-intervals come up together, recall the first five-minute intervals, then the fifteen-minute intervals, and then the forty-five-minute intervals. Write on the board the list of intervals:

immediate
1 minute
3–5 minutes

12–20 minutes
45–60 minutes
3 hours or end of day

To use this method regularly, obtain three timers and set one at one minute, one at five, and one at fifteen minutes. Cognitive styles may relate to the task slightly differently. Auditory students emphasize talking out a capsule as though hearing it on headphones a word at a time and kinesthetics may add analogical body movement or imagine doing so.

Chapter Six

Focus Learning

A few considerations can aid our choices about focusing the manner and content of students' thinking.

39. USE MAPS

Be conscious of your map for learning. Imagine a family planning a vacation to the Grand Canyon. Later, smart kid number two sees his father looking at a map of New England and says, "Dad, why are you looking at New England if we're going to the Grand Canyon?" The direction of focus should be the direction for action.

We can think of maps as directions channeling behavior, internal representations sequencing upcoming actions. Learning a map adjusts our thoughts to proceed accordingly. When students' maps generate problems, we need one ourselves to return them to cooperation. We first install thinking that makes desired action at least possible (they know what to do) and then that makes it easy and pleasant (assured success with a positive emotional tone).

The power of a mental map to organize learning was illustrated by Dan who had had difficulties in his life, turned a corner, and was doing well in a job. He had spent several months at an employment center to raise his skills and described his first math class.

> This big group was sitting there. None of us had done well in school. The teacher comes in and the first thing he says is, "Okay, who can tell me how to calculate the square root of 64?" He stared at us, looking from one to another. We all lowered our heads and thought, "Uh oh. This is going to be bad." After

> a long silence, he says, "Alright, I'll tell you. The answer is A, B, C." He wrote on the board A, B, C and said, "It's only one step and another step and another step. And this is what you need to remember. Every single problem you meet is exactly the same, just A, B, C." And that's the way he taught us so that everybody learned. Every problem just boiled down to A, B, C. All math was just a series of steps, and we learned the steps.

With this map for reading other maps, students gained confidence that they could learn a subject that had intimidated them.

Like the math teacher, transmit the map before you ask for the behavior. If the steps are A and B and C, develop ABC in their minds as a unit. Without it, action is hesitant and harder to coordinate. The larger the number affected by an activity, the clearer the map must be. Without maps for new behaviors, students tend to act randomly or return to old habits.

Become aware of how you formulate what you want to accomplish. You might frame your purpose as students exerting constant, stimulating effort. Imagine you are a coach, and everything depends on managing effort and attitude.

With your goal clear, two other tools are essential. One is the ability to observe sensitively whether or not you are getting what you want. You must see and hear accurately the activity in front of you to determine your current results. If you misread the situation, your strategy is sure to misfire. Your second tool is your set of flexible responses for how to manage what you encounter, all the methods you have learned as a teacher.[25]

It may help you to put words to what you notice. This helps to activate the link between outer events and your possible responses. Perhaps today you want them to talk to each other better. Seeing them in animated involvement, you voice thoughts to yourself:

> Ah, I see some skills used. Good! There's attention to each other, and a brief silence over there. He's thinking about what someone said. And these three are commenting on the same topic! They've had four sentences now on the same issue with no one veering off. Good going. I can let them proceed a few minutes more. I'll talk to Jeremy later about interrupting.

Where your map asks for accurate sensing, you (1) notice behavior carefully and (2) describe advances in skill you observe. Your flexible responses then (3) offer accurate feedback, (4) shape by giving guidelines, and (5) welcome their perceptions of their progress.

Create an Expectation

To initiate a plan, post something, announce something, make a prediction, begin preparations, or confer about arrangements: "Can you move your desks? Turn and face this way. We're doing something new today."

Pointing them toward pending action awakens an action set, stimulating neurologically the capacities they will employ. Teach the map before asking for the behavior. Cooperating in learning the map forecasts that they will follow it. Their unconscious receives a suggestion, "You're going to do this, so get ready." Later you call on the map and discover your prophetic accuracy. There they are, doing what they had in mind to do.

Project ahead: "We're going to start this on Wednesday." Outline their steps. Noticing everyone learning them ahead puts group consensus to work. As you supply details, everyone appears to agree, implying that they will too.

The activity must be clear. A kindergarten teacher receives 100% cooperation on a four-step map: "Everyone gets a piece of cake if you do four things: One, take a napkin. Two, put a piece of cake on it. Three, return to your seat. Four, eat the cake at your seat. I want everyone to learn the four steps before anyone takes a piece of cake." Try to make your maps just as clear, maybe with boxes on the board, steps 1, 2, and 3.

Our map for their learning goes beyond steps posted on the board, however. We want it in their minds as an idea so that they need only look within to guide their actions. Then you free them to follow it, relinquishing control, "tossing the ball" entirely to them so they can draw on the idea you delivered rather than react to you.

Watch what happens and confer later: How did it go? What went right? What diverged from the guideline? What should we change? Clarify the map and run the action again: "If the cake falls on the floor, go to the closet, get the dustpan and broom . . . ."

Regard failure to follow a map as a learning issue. If some students do not comply, proceed as if they will come around. At first all you ask is that they learn the steps of the map. Many are willing to watch someone else apply it yet this is still aligned to your purpose. That they sit and watch the group till they understand presumes hesitation from uncertainty rather than from any negative quality. In truth they are not yet able to mesh with the activity—often due to their uncertainty about their place in the group, self-image, or fears of failure. Another detour leading to cooperation is asking them to collect information with an observer's checklist and report what they see.

Demonstrate the map. Sometimes showing is easier than explaining. Bring several students in front of everyone, give them directions, walk them through the map, correct them as needed, ask others what they observed, and explain what else they should notice. A two-minute demonstration may do better than reexplaining the map.

Transition Time

When only repeated prompts obtain their attention, you need a new map. At first your students may require tight control to manage them, may cooperate only gradually upon being coaxed and corrected, may be suspicious of new activities, wish not to be bothered, and self-discipline may be alien to them. Counteracting these habits, you do not want your exasperated plea, "Could we please get it quiet in here?" to signal them to pay attention to you.

Change occurs from managing certain details. If we want a precise behavior, we have no choice but to attend to the variables involved. No teacher takes pleasure in being picky, but we have to pattern student behavior. A parallel is teaching children to wash dishes. You cannot escape from insisting on the details you want them to attend to until their map incorporates them spontaneously. If students waste the class's time, you attend to details redirecting them.

Change is harder when based on personal pressure. They react differently to it than to their own map. "Coming down on a student" implies giving up on his ability to think and that instead you must exert power over him, converting your exchange into a struggle. Delivering a map means believing in better behavior through ideas understood and agreed on.

Collecting evidence of a need is a good step to forming a map. Evidence shows that this is not just you being cranky. You time repeated delays with a stopwatch, quantifying to the second the time they waste in transitions. Setting an activity in motion, you might say:

> I'd like to let you work together more. I think you might enjoy it and help each other, but there's a problem. It requires changing from one activity (#1 on the board) to another (#2) without wasting time. You'll get up, move to a partner, and begin talking with each other. In doing so, it's easy to get off the subject. If you're going to work together, you need to be able to shift directly from learning individually to learning with partners. We need to see how quickly you can make that change, and then change back when the activity ends. So to practice doing this more efficiently, first I'll explain what to do. Then I'll raise the timer, say "Go," and start the timer. You begin to carry out the plan. We'll keep track of the time it takes you to change from one activity to another, and then try to improve on it.

You give them a clear map of what to do, signals that start and end it, and time the portion you want to improve. They rise, go to their partner, sit together, and ask and answer the questions. Time them from when you say "Begin" to when you see everyone engaged.

Toward the end of the period, say, "Class, would you please end in a half-minute?" and in thirty seconds say "Please return to your seats." Time them from when you make the request to when they fulfill it.

Make a map for your own versatile response. If their group work deteriorates, your map about yourself guides. Read their dysfunction as a message about their needs rather than about negative qualities: "They really need clear ideas to go by, don't they!" Notice yourself interpreting the situation in a way that restores you to selecting an effective response.

If you cannot generate a proactive direction, you can always retreat temporarily. After unsuccessful small group discussions, say (1) "Well, let's end for today. Everyone seems a little distracted." (2) The next day, return just to teaching the map: "Let's make sure everyone understands this and has it in mind. Remember the guidelines. Go over them with your partner and clarify any you don't understand." (3) Initiate the activity as you see cooperation in learning the map: "Congratulations! Everyone learned those steps faster than I expected. So we have some time now to do the activity today. Here are your groups . . . ." As they use time well, (4) add more: "Everyone did so well yesterday that I'm going to add an extra five minutes. If your group ends early, take out some personal reading." (5) You might offer an appropriate incentive such as self-managed time they can save up or a reward they would like to work toward together (cf. Bonus Time in 28. Use Consequences).

Your map for responding to noncooperation includes (1) recognizing need instead of opposition, (2) reality-checking by gathering information, (3) shifting to a positive attitude, (4) examining alternatives to find the most constructive, and (5) taking specific action. Like a strategy in sports, students need a plan, a signal that says "Go," and action operating the plan: one, two, three. They like themselves better when their energy is focused and flows smoothly. They are like soldiers: Who will prepare himself for battle if the trumpet sounds an uncertain note?

40. DEGREES OF PRECISION

Distinguish three levels of exactness and use the appropriate one for the task at hand.

Exact Basics

For beginners, these are the names of things and facts about the world. Adults learn countless ideas exactly: observations of the physical world, scientific and mathematical formulas and measurement systems, basic vocabulary and grammar, and terms for any discipline. Here also are structural elements, parts and wholes, and fundamental principles discovered by centuries of investigation.

Because both their selection and form are already settled and must be assimilated as they are, this learning offers precise conclusion. We can know it completely at the level that concerns us now, and mastery of it enlarges our creative ability. The formula for the area of a circle and that *hablar* means "to talk" in Spanish apply to all circles and all instances of speaking in Spanish. Where learning is clearly identified and unanimously regarded as necessary, exact mastery is the basis for all later knowledge.

Elaborated Applications

This adds specifics to the prior level: examples of formulas, uses of words, instances of a generalization, details supporting basic ideas, and the reasons, evidence, and principles generating an insight. In this area, the form depends on something more exact already learned, but the selection of details varies. Elementary students studying the formula for the area of a rectangle have unlimited variables for different size rectangles. A foreign language vocabulary yields an endless variety of ideas drawing on the same word meanings.

Completeness for this zone is defined arbitrarily. Students might do 150 long-division problems at varying degrees of difficulty before the method is mastered. Competence with a foreign language vocabulary word might be achieved with fluid use in five contexts.

Narrative Extension

This knowledge incorporates the entire world of experience. Where an issue may be viewed from many angles, the selection and form of learning varies with the current purpose. Think of history, geography, psychology, interpersonal dynamics, entertainment, literature, art, anthropology, personalized learning, and creativity. Beyond their exact basics, one can be right in many ways with no natural boundaries. Because every piece of knowledge can be connected potentially to others, teachers may reasonably allow students to set their own priorities and help them obtain as much of this knowledge as time allows. There is no impelling reason to teach everyone the same thing if they simply learn and can demonstrate something.

Understanding the difference between these levels helps guide students' practice. It is a tedious mistake to expect the same exactness in level two and three material that level one requires. And it is as egregious an error to leave the variance in level one material easily accommodated in level three. Knowledge at levels two and three can be shifted and changed. Freezing it tends to march the mind in set tracks, but flexibility with level one material courts disaster. Rocket seals need to fit, parts must articulate and train crossing lights work; the surgeon's knife must cut exactly, and speaker and listener should derive the same meaning from a word.

An eighth grade boy with dyslexia reading at the third grade illustrated the levels. For years he had endured labels, special classes, and fruitless attempts to help him while his anger and discouragement deepened. Trying him at various reading tasks and watching him closely for a few days, I discovered that no one had ever taught him the vowel sounds needed to decipher words. For eight years in the public system, no one had addressed this need. In a couple weeks of practicing these exactly (level one) and applying them to simple words under my oversight (level two), he took off. Year-end tests showed him covering five years of reading in a year (level three).

Similar was an intelligent fifth grade boy struggling with aspects of first grade math. Taking him through microsteps of simple problems and examining his thought processes, I found that for years he had been confused about the difference between multiply and divide. Exact basics must be taught exactly.

41. SAVE BASICS

From the body of information presented, extract the synthesis, key fact, or element of structure you want them to save, the core jewel worth the extra effort to carry it forward.

Terms

If you use new terms they do not understand to explain concepts they do not understand, they learn both by rote at best. Compile terms into a meaningful set. An upper elementary math glossary may contain 200 terms, mastery of which you can spread through a year. Include the rules associated with each one's use, its order in any sequence or formula, and problems that employ it. Plot their progress visibly with a Content Scoreboard (cf. 47), a column for each category of terms.

Structure

The structure of a subject is probably the easiest way to understand everything else about it. Diagram it, and check whether your text's table of contents is the optimal arrangement (cf. 35). When you can, leave it to them to select what else to master. Beyond the terms and structure essential for their grade level, a spectrum of knowledge might be valid. Check whether they understand it, put it into a form to master, and master it. Once they understand how to apply their effort, let them manage more of it. For everyone to work on something different they need only arrange it by Q and A, practice it, and score it.

Experiences, physical activity, or hands-on aspects link their sensory system to the less tangible, making associated ideas easier to absorb: handling measuring devices, assembling pieces, bodily movement, or use of tools. Narrating the behaviors of gathering information can make it easier to retain. Field notes can be rewritten, shared, and explained back and forth. Work products, experiments, exploration, and lab work can be documented with a personal logbook showing date, place, activity, results, and time spent, and then organized as Q and A.

Easy Details

Pausing briefly to recall who said what in a discussion can help them capture alternate perspectives. Remembering how individuals responded to a topic fills in an overall summary. Episodes, events, physical activity, sequences, raw data, and imaginative images stick readily in the mind.

If ensuring success for all concerns you, use material easy for everyone to absorb including those finding it hard to read or write. Draw from multisensory presentations, video- or CD-based lessons, or programs by Nature, Nova, or National Geographic. Often service activities contain a learning residue. Ask students to identify a question that elicits it and the points or steps that summarize it. Projects usually comprise steps that can be narrated.

The use of audiovisual sources changes slightly when you want assimilated knowledge instead of entertainment or familiarization. Assimilating means chewing one bite and swallowing it before taking another bite—permanence with something rather than coverage of everything. Working with CDs, DVDs, videos, or audio tapes, avoid the temptation to finish them quickly since they typically present too much to absorb in one sitting.

Install the important points from one segment at a time. The rest will spend the night safely in its jacket, ready to be more stimulating the next day: (1) Take notes and identify questions while students watch or listen. (2) Halt the tape every ten to fifteen minutes. (3) Present a question about that section, pause for everyone to recall, and draw a name randomly to answer. (4) Do this with all the points from that portion. (5) They close their eyes and run it in their mind. (6) As time allows, they record the summary questions and answers in their notebooks. (7) They tell them to a partner.

42. LEARN EVERYTHING

Ignorance surrounds us but a world of knowledge awaits. All of it, I believe, should be welcome at school and not just minimal course requirements. We want each student to graduate a polymath.

Start with a large question and fill it in gradually. You might organize thirteen years by dividing the universe of knowledge into, say, fifty subjects like science, mathematics, language, literature, foreign language, politics, economics, religion, philosophy, environment, anthropology, psychology, geology, ecology, community, sports, business, biography, health, family, home economics, learning methods, personal development, fiction, the arts (culture, music, art, theater), history (world, American, regional), and the world today.

Include subjects of local interest like ethnic studies, the history and literature of different cultures, flora and fauna, coastlines, mountains, desert, industry, agriculture, resource extraction, and occupations unique to the area. Expect them every year to save what they learned before, add to every category, and tell about each entire field with a comprehensive explanation: "Tell all you know about geography," "Tell all you know about government," and "Tell all you know about health." They begin their answer with the structure of the subject, divide it into chunks and sub-chunks, and explain each.

They practice telling it to each other. When teachers must ask all the questions themselves, the time they can spend with each student is limited, prohibiting long answers. Hearing out one student would monopolize an entire period while most waited. The problem is like a Grand Coulee Dam with only one pipe for water to pass through. The solution is more pipes. We enlist half the class to listen to the other half.

Varied questions about it make knowledge more flexible. Having written a paragraph on the board, you can ask, "What question is this the answer to?" They suggest alternatives and pick one. As they grow, they need to recognize better the questions to which life itself will provide answers.

Integrate piecemeal information into larger questions. Often pieces come from fill-in blanks, questions and answers at the ends of chapters, and definitions. In subjects like science that require exact mastery of bits, you may at first teach single points answering single questions. A stream of them can involve everyone with small doses of success, and demonstrate to students with low confidence that they can learn.

We do not want to sacrifice understanding. Explaining proceeds up a continuum of complexity as students integrate bits into longer answers. Questions about rules for commas, capitalizations, and sentence structure can be combined: "As though you were teaching the class, tell what you know about rules of grammar, give examples of each, and when and why you would use them." The effort nudges students to grasp individual ideas by where they belong in a synthesis.

You might think at first, "I don't have time for that." If not, you use the time for something else. What, exactly, is more important than integrated, articulate knowledge? What are they spending time on instead? If you show them how to gather basic information efficiently, they will have time to develop further mental skills.

Answer Expansion

Students stay invested in old knowledge better as they combine it with new. The two together make revising more effective. Changes occur in the region of the mid brain used for motivation and reward processing.[26]

Assign individuals to find more about something already learned: "When we review your question, we'll ask you what you've found for us." They can explore sources and uncover details others can add to their notes. Enlarging and restructuring answers stimulates flexibility and assimilation.[27]

As students add new material, they can insert sheets in their notebooks at the appropriate places. If they score what they learn, new material may not alter the form of prior knowledge. They can increase their score on that question without reexplaining previous material.

43. DIVIDE SUBJECTS

When they are able to gather and organize knowledge by themselves, you can let them divide the labor and share the results. Each learns a piece and teaches it to others. You might assign this over a single period, a day, or in longer work. It can be done in pairs, organization groups, or other teams you configure.

One at a time in their group they lay on the table the questions and answers they wrote out and explain them. Others clarify, offer their insights, add ideas from other sources, summarize the contributions, and copy them into their notebooks. The group then might use pairs to practice explaining what they have collected or defer practice to another day.

Using a multitext approach, you can either stop at the point that each one gathers information for themselves or can arrange for them to exchange it. In the first case, (1) assign each student a specific source or let them select it. (2) They develop notes on their Answers pages with matching questions on their Questions pages, and (3) practice explaining the answer to a partner along with their other learning, and (4) score it.

In the second case, they (1) identify the information they want to share, (2) write a Q and A summary others can copy, (3) in pairs or groups share what they learned, (4) copy each other's summaries, (5) practice the new learning with a partner, and (6) score it.

44. FOCUS ON PROGRESS

Everyone would like to focus on progress instead of deficit, but "catching them doing it right" is easy to violate. We feel obligated to point out errors, and their errors then become our negative measure of the student.[28] Here instead we mark progress entirely through successes.

One teacher noted rapid benefit from crediting her special needs students with all the new, correct answers they could add to prior assignments. They were incredulous at first because raising their scores felt to them like cheating, but her value was on more correct answers. She let them add as much new material as they were willing to undertake. When they realized that she was not mistake-oriented, they lost their fear of being penalized and began to enjoy school more.

One group of high school students were so negative and unpredictable that they had been bounced from public school, and interruptions, ridicule, and rudeness were common. Their teacher created a large chart. In columns across the top she listed eight communication skills with students' names down the side, and without explanation began giving them a tally mark for using a skill in class.

They noticed quickly and began to congratulate themselves and then others. At first they did so jokingly, she said, but soon became serious about it. When she felt hurried and failed to record the tallies, the students asked her to continue them. When she allowed them to tally each other's use of skills, they complied enthusiastically, going to the chart at the end of small group work or during class discussions. She soon saw improvement in their personal relationships, communications, and sense of play.

Students respond better when the behaviors scored are observable and objective, and do not depend on others' judgment such as: look at speaker, wait till other finishes, use others' names respectfully, use others' words and ideas respectfully, remember what others say, give compliments, thank people, and tell what helped you.

If you include your own name among those scored, you encourage them to notice your modeling. Since the first two skills occur spontaneously as students interact with friends, positive marks can accumulate quickly. You might also say, "When there is no more than one person there, you can go up and give anyone a tally." This can be tied to reward systems in lock-down schools or in classes for those with emotional or behavioral problems. Teachers and students can award tokens accumulated for prizes, food, or privileges.

Adapt for Learning Disabilities

Although many students with an identified disability are in special education classes, some in the mainstream also find an aspect of learning hard, usually how they take in information. Once they have it, they may demonstrate superior retention and understanding. To make this initial step easier, try not to burden it with fluff. Ask them to learn only what you truly want them to keep, so that they do not work hard to learn what they will discard anyway.

Find each one's open door and include it in the sequence everyone uses: see pictures of it, hear a description of it, write it down, speak it to a partner, speak it to the class, imagine it, repeat it, and give it structure. If you can include each one's strength in the format everyone uses, all learn.[29]

Deliver knowledge no faster than the pace at which they install it. (1) Transmit small segments written and summarized, (2) followed at once by Partner Practice to explain them, and (3) regular use of the Peg List to keep them fresh. Once they have a chunk inside them, reinforce it further by (4) Mental Movie and (5) Impromptu Performance, and (6) resynthesize it as new elements are added.

Individualized strategies can help. A student who finds the physical act of writing hard might for a time dictate to a parent or classmate. Another may need to stand and act out or symbolize the material physically. Verbal expression means more to some. When they have more to learn than they can process, handouts and notes copied from other students may accommodate them.

Chapter Seven

Replace Grading with Scoring

Scores are a way to mark successful completion of effort. Here we examine problems with standard grading and how scoring by points of knowledge and time explaining can improve the evaluation of students' progress and stimulate them.

45. REPLACE GRADING WITH SCORING

Solving a problem usually depends on asking the right question. When progress seems bogged down in struggle, we are encouraged to examine our question.

We need to assume first that adult authorities ultimately want what enables students to learn best. We ask that question first, ahead of our attempt to assess the results of our method. When we know our horse is sick, it violates common sense to measure how fast he pulls the cart. First we heal the horse and then figure out how to evaluate his speed.

About students, we inquire, "Do we take them optimally to the next step of their learning sequence?" We examine our design for students' activities until we get it right. Once that works well, we turn to the second question of "How fast?" if it still matters to us. We do not want to answer the second question in a way that obstructs our primary goal.

Attempting to define students' effort with grades has proven unsatisfactory.[30] This is inevitable because grades do not fix learning at any consistent point on its trajectory from total ignorance to complete mastery. Of two students in different schools tested on identical material, one faces multiple-choice and true-false questions answered in five minutes whereas the other gives a detailed summary taking forty-five minutes. Both qualify for an A grade, but we can guess which probably knows more. The fifteen steps here comprise what we might term "Signals of the depth of knowledge."

With no common standard, one teacher takes steps four and five as A grade work whereas another places it at step twelve.

1. Student is present in class, sits still, and looks at you when you talk.
2. Student recognizes "Yes, we had that!"
3. Student sorts a preposterous from a plausible answer.
4. Student does sentence completion and fill-in blanks.
5. Student improves on fifty-fifty chance with a true-false answer.
6. Student picks the right answer from a set of four.
7. Student matches columns of associated terms.
8. Student answers in a single word with coaching.
9. Student answers in a single sentence with coaching.
10. Student answers in a single sentence without help.
11. Student gives a multipart answer without help.
12. Student comprehensively explains structure, terms, and details having just looked at the answer.
13. Student gives answer 12 having last looked at it yesterday.
14. Student gives answer 12 having last looked at it a week ago.
15. Student gives answer 12 having last looked at it six months ago.

Learning carries forward an impression in the mind. If the mind must rely on help as in the first nine steps, it fails to sustain the learning under its own power. Impressions remain on the surface of the mind.

The scoring I suggest counts increments of continuous, conscious learning that has crossed the critical threshold. It is independently retained by the mind as in the last six steps of the continuum. It presumes that estimating the depth of learning prior to that point is a waste of time. If what matters is what sticks, we measure it when it least does that and hold it to that standard. When a student identifies a piece of knowledge and consciously practices and assimilates it, he or she can count it, score it, claim it, post it, carry it forward, accumulate it, present it, and easily make it permanent by periodic attention to it.[31]

Such scoring offers several benefits: It averts disputes. Parents are less likely to complain about scores than about grades. A track and field score just says, "This is how high your child jumped," or "This is your child's time in the race." Period. We only want to represent accurately what the child did: "Your child got twenty correct out of twenty-five." Period.

It focuses effort. Scoring makes games possible and appealing as an orderly, objective demonstration of skill. No need to trouble ourselves with how someone sees it. The score says it all, a platoon of influences expressed in one number. The score does not describe the skills drawn on but rather marks their excellence. We mobilize attention and determination, accomplish the task, achieve the score, and feel refreshed and satisfied.

It enhances students' control. Their points are not compared to an abstract standard. Scoring correlates their effort with their progress without needing to please anyone, guess what others think, or worry about how they are perceived. They realize, "I got fifteen answers and I'm going for sixteen." They know exactly what their score is and others register it the same way.

They experience more freedom. Nothing keeps them in a mold except their effort. Scoring provides tight feedback between intent and outcome even in a few minutes. Their first score of an increment does not mean that they have mastered it, but they have surmounted the crucial boundary of explaining it without help and can foresee continuing to meet the same criterion. If the knowledge disappears and the student can no longer explain it, the score drops proportionately.

Scores present a direct proportion between the amount of effort, the amount of learning, and the resulting score. Effort lines up behind certified results and initial results grow to higher levels. Without accurate measures, energy along the continuum of effort loses aim, and competence is less easily verified.

Instant scoring motivates more. Students are most ready for feedback about their effort right after it is completed. Energy is caught at its greatest receptivity, pointing them to their next burst of effort: "You got it! Now go to the next."

The motivational juice in the link between effort and results drops when validation of results is delayed. When someone tells us, "I'll check on you in a half-hour," we work harder than if they say "I'll check on you at the end of the month." Immediacy of feedback stimulates immediate effort. Specificity of scoring motivates specific effort.

Scoring can accommodate graded material. If you use grades instead of scoring the quantity of knowledge mastered, you might post the number of answer points maintained till the end of the term that earn a grade; 300 points might be an A, 250 a B, and 200 a C. If you wish to use scoring primarily, you can still incorporate assignments that do not lend themselves to a score. Assigning a report for practice in researching, organizing, and writing, you might say "Your basic score for this semester depends on the points and time of material you master. For this report, though, you can receive up to 100 points more, depending on the effort you put into it." Your criteria determine the numerical score you give their work.

46. SCORE BY POINTS AND TIME

Scoring by points and time aligns effort with signals of success. Regardless of the type of activity involved, humans seem to want to know what their effort obtains for them. When their motivation is uncertain or weak, an obvious aid we can supply is establishing a perfect correlation between effort and success.

Score by Points

Scoring by points works best in academic knowledge that has discrete parts to learn: days of a week, 7; rules for commas, 11; names of muscles, 240. Each part is a specific chunk of knowledge. To assign points to knowledge not cleanly divided into parts, think of an essay question on a test. You look for ideas you expect to be there, perhaps five or six. The score you give counts up points the answer supplies (in addition to other characteristics you wish to teach—cf. prior section). The student maintains the score by maintaining the answer.

In general we grant a point of score if a piece contains knowledge not made clear or explained elsewhere, with no half-score for a half-point. A point is a coherent thought expressed in a sentence or clause, its size determined by what readily hangs together at the class's level of understanding.

A way to identify points is by what you consider mistakes. What could go wrong at this level is what to measure when it goes right. What you mark off if missed on a test is an increment deserving a score when gained. As their work improves, something changes. Count the new thing their effort adds.

Incomplete knowledge can be vague or partial. Vague is undefined. Students may "have the idea" enough to recognize or guess at it, a kind less useful to them. Partial knowledge may still be boundaried, understood, and retained well though incomplete, credited as the number of sub-points told back correctly without help, such as four of seven. The four are definite. The listener records them on the score line under (or beside) the question in the speaker's notebook and initials it. Partial knowledge points them toward completing the set while vague knowledge leaves them uncertain what to do.

Assign scores to parts independently understood. To prepare for a trip to the airport, second graders learn parts of an airplane, naming those pointed out in a picture. The second stage is to tell the function of each part. Identifying and counting tells you the extent of the remaining task: "I have all seventeen parts named!" "Wonderful! Now learn what they do." Seventeen points learned, seventeen to go.

Students can help you. A high school student who caught on to this laid out the factoring of a polynomial in sixteen steps. "Is this what you had in mind?" he asked, taking the teacher through the steps. Breaking a lengthy process into steps assures that each is correct.

Score by Time

Most students are reassured by using points first because they define a task exactly, but many subjects are understood better through a narrative. Assembling scattered pieces into a coherent arrangement gives a better grasp of the whole. In literature, each step of a plot, literary element, or character can be learned as a point of knowledge but then scored further in an integrated explanation.

The time they talk is a measure of their effort. A student was clocked for nineteen minutes explaining the chemistry of the sun from a TV special the night before. Time can measure mastery of many subjects containing a mass of details all equally valid. Studying the Civil War, one student may have a six-minute explanation. In a thirty-six-minute explanation, another student has read, practiced, and accumulated significant understanding. Then you discover a three-hour-and-nineteen-minute explanation from a student who loves the subject and fascinates others.

One might ask why bother to time answers to the second. The reason is because it matters. It declares, "Even seconds of your knowledge count." They paid for it with their effort and would like to know their return on investment.

A clue to the significance even of seconds is how our culture esteems quantified effort toward goals possessing no intrinsic value. Most games and sports amount to an arbitrary accounting of effort and skill. We piggyback on this presumption yet provide the intrinsic benefit of life knowledge to boot. Our use of scoring draws on a mind-set students use extensively to authenticate their progress.

Combine points and time into a single score at the rate of four points per minute and express it either way, based on the estimate that in a minute one speaks about four points of knowledge. If in a week a student earns 36 points plus 16 minutes time, we multiply the minutes by 4. In 16 minutes, one would cover approximately 64 points: $16 \times 4 = 64$. Then we add these to the points already counted up: $64 + 36 = 100$ points. To express the same score as time, we divide the 36 points by 4: $36 / 4 = 9$, and add these to the timed minutes: $9 + 16 = 25$-minute score.

If time is used alone, ask them to get the answer smoothly in mind before presenting it to a partner for scoring. You might introduce a subject and have students practice it initially on Monday. They reexplain it on Tuesday, and score it for the record on Wednesday. If repetition, hesitance, vagueness, or padding with irrelevant information occurs, listeners reduce the score proportionately.

Personal characteristics may affect timing. Students' scores for the same material may not match exactly. Some speak slower and some faster. Some with many words say a little and others use few words to say a lot. The adult world values both elaboration and conciseness, and we want students able to do either. What matters is how a change in their score signals their effort to accumulate fresh knowledge while maintaining the prior knowledge.

Standardize the recording of questions. The notebook arrangement suggested (cf. 1) helps you know each question's stage of development; first that it is complete with all pieces correct, and later that it is permanent. Scoring focuses practice by telling how much of the information has reached the criterion of explainability without help.

Let's say that in Language Arts a student has been reading *War and Peace*, and in his Questions page accounts for his time narrating the contents of the book:

24. What is the story of *War and Peace* by Tolstoy?

4:30t LB/ 19:10t TL/ 1:12:43t AS

The score line says that in his first attempt at summarizing the book, listener L. B. timed him for four-and-a-half minutes. His second attempt was nineteen minutes and ten seconds, timed by student T. L. After he read to the end of the book, his third attempt was timed by a student or family member with the initials A. S. for one hour, twelve minutes, and forty-three seconds.

For adapting practice to the shorter times available in a classroom, you might divide a book into separate questions about chapters, plot line, key events, philosophy expressed, cultural and environmental elements, character development, and relationships between characters.

In the sciences, questions 32, 73, and 74 might appear as:

32. Define 13 terms related to fish on page 350 of Life Science text [13].

9p KS/ 13p LT

For questions scored by points, the bracketed numbers at the end of a question tell the number of points in a complete answer if known, to help the student aim for task completion. She first recited nine of thirteen terms to someone with the initials K. S. Later to a listener initialed L. T. she demonstrated mastery of them all.

73. Name and explain ten factors that affect the climate [10].

5p PR/ 8p KS/ 10p KS

After this student gathered and wrote out the ten factors answering the question, he told back five of them to another initialed P. R. Student K. S. heard eight and then ten on two occasions. In the next question the student might draw on the same information with a narrative explanation for an added score:

74. Explain the circulation of the atmosphere.

30t RG/ 1:45t FL/ 3:10t AS

The student incorporated some of the information from question 73 into question 74, and expanded it to three minutes ten seconds after an initial explanation of a half-minute. The presence of the colon (and absence of "p" for points) indicates a timed answer. Students may wish to add a "t" for the latter.

49. Give three rules and examples for order of operations [6].

3p RT/ 4p AS/ 6p LT

This score might indicate any combination of rules and examples that totaled three at first, then four, then all six possible.

If a question arises about what time score to apply to a portion of learning, be guided by the effort involved. If they wish to score a new piece that appears to you a retooling of something already learned, ask "What new effort resulted in this learning?" For more examples of scoring by points, cf. 54.

Clarify Level of Detail

It often happens that as students practice explaining a section, their answers become shorter. They are more efficient with the same knowledge, their fluidity a sign of mastery. A competent person can recast knowledge, talking either at length or with a brief summary as needed. To stabilize an explanation so it renders a consistent score, you might suggest your own words as a model: "Say what I would in presenting it, along with diagrams, examples, and illustrations." Or, "Think how you would tell it to a younger brother or sister so they could understand it." Or, "If a new person came to class who didn't know this material and you were assigned to help him catch up, what would you say?"

If they can demonstrate a masterful explanation in less time than previously measured, there is no need to reduce their score unless it represents knowledge lost. We assume that most could use up extra words to expand time if required to.

47. SCOREBOARDS

Because we wish never to embarrass or discourage students, we weigh carefully how we may stress them. Our manner of assessment should not discourage their effort. Being judged by an authority figure, for example, is stressful for anyone. Because it represents another's opinion of them, it can leave them feeling diminished. Their own opinion of the opinion can multiply their discomfort.

Motivation is sustained better from counting up increments mastered, even posting hourly progress on a classroom chart (cf. Appendix 7). Doing so depends on the teacher defining increments of learning clearly enough that specific effort registers success. When a number acknowledging their effort appears, children's body language reveals their pleasure. They are glad to know their accomplishment, win or lose.

They like measures that are fair, can change over time and often quickly, apply to something they have control over, and respond directly to their effort. They are not helpless before a teacher's displeasure, nor set aside because of race, status, or past academics, nor zeroed out by others more capable. Their achievement has its own substance that they can increase by more effort.

A few questions may help you weigh the benefits of scoring:

1. Does the system extend something already familiar? Starting from kindergarten, scoring can convey complete success for everyone. If some take a little longer to achieve it or others add more points, no matter.
2. Does the score give them information they can use? The Content Scoreboard (cf. below) helps them monitor accumulated learning, gain clues from others' scores, and make choices about directing their effort.
3. Is the score under their control? Their score presents an exact proportion between their effort at practice and the knowledge they gain.
4. Is the score accurate? It must reliably reflect their gains.
5. Is it comparative or personalized? Grades "on the curve" may stimulate those of comparable ability but discourage others too different. As people's posted scores vary, the teacher can explain the value to emphasize:

> Let's say two students are reading. One finds three points she wants to save, writes them down, and practices them. Another finds one point to save, and thinks about it. He writes it down and practices explaining it. Are the three points better than the one? (Let them think about this and offer their views.) Really, we don't know. The one point the second student saves may be very valuable to him later. It may guide his life, while the first student may forget about the three points. The scores just help each one keep track of their own progress. They know how much more knowledge they have today than yesterday. How they use it later is up to them. For now, we just want everyone to learn something well. You will choose later how valuable it is to you.

6. Is it group-oriented or individual? Twenty in a class might aim for 120 points total rather than six points each. You monitor and post their collective achievement. Students know their own contribution but are often stimulated by a collective target.
7. Are they expending effort? If you are confident that the energy they expend accounts for their accomplishment and that they benefit from an objective record of it, they will believe that also. Their progress from any starting point depends not on ability or opinion but on steady effort. If you believe instead that ability is the variable—which you can do nothing about—you are tempted unconsciously to dismiss a student.

If effort matters, they look to you to guide it. Share the story of the tortoise and the hare, about perseverance. Tell them about Professor K. Anders Ericsson of Florida State University. He was curious how people at the top of their field were different from others. It was not by intelligence, he found. Their IQ typically matched that of the average college student. Setting them apart instead were thousands of hours more practice than average performers in their field. Practice "made perfect."[32]

Points Scoreboard

To keep track of students' points of knowledge, Appendix 7 offers a template with columns for days of the week, a cumulative total at the end, and rows for student names. Cover it with acetate or enter scores with a soft-lead pencil easy to erase. Post their daily scores under the appropriate column, and add them up weekly for a growing total. Maintain your own copy of the chart in case students enter incorrect data or tamper with the chart. Numerical scores count up the points of knowledge students demonstrate to each other by telling them back without help.

This chart design works well scoring with points only. If time is used also, the two are coalesced into a single point score daily until Friday when they are added to the cumulative total. Once they understand how to use the chart, they prefer to post their scores with their partner hour by hour, increasing their day's total. They can also turn them in to you or to a student you assign to post them.

Maintain the standard that only real numbers are worth posting, verified by a partner. Monitor their accuracy by listening in while students explain them, by frequent Impromptu Performances and by switching partners.

Points and Time Scoreboard

To accommodate regular use of both points and time, see the second template in Appendix 7. Across the top, label columns as daily and cumulative time, daily and cumulative points, and a combined total expressed as either points or time (cf. 46).

At the end of a period or day, students hand you a slip of paper with (1) their name, (2) the number of points or time they gained, and (3) the name of the student who signed off on their count. Daily points can either be added to the total throughout the day or penciled on the chart hourly and added at day's end. Erase scores from a prior column when combining them into a cumulative or total column.

Soon after introducing her class to the scoreboard idea, a high school teacher said, "We're charting all kinds of things now!" Visibility lends significance, such as by displaying class scoreboards in a hallway, each with a line chart for their total progress in learning, or listed together on a single chart with columns for their weekly accumulated points.

Content Scoreboard

Besides displaying scores, scoreboards can organize content. In elementary classes, post a large erasable version of the blank chart in Appendix 6. Teach the comma and semicolon by writing each use at the head of a column with student names down the side. When a student learns one of the uses, place an X in that column beside his or her name. When everyone learns the entire series, erase it and divide the parts of a different learning task among the column headings. As their pace picks up, cycle the content daily. Track any subject by organizing answers into parts they can cross off as they learn them one by one.

In high school science, imagine yourself a biology teacher with a 700-page text in twenty-six chapters. Beyond your few priorities, you welcome anything they learn from the book. On the erasable chart (Appendix 6), write a chapter number in each of the columns across the top and student names down the side. Students then post a count of the points they learn under each chapter.

You increase permanent learning just by asking them to maintain their point scores to the end of the term, A student might note that he has only one point in Chapter 6, and in the minutes till the end of a period decides to pick up a few more. He reads briefly, writes notes on his Answers page, records a question, and has two more points in Chapter 6 on track to mastery. Next day he explains them to a partner who certifies them for posting.

Students might jump ahead to any chapter that interests them and share with others what they find. This familiarizes them with the subject's structure, allows them to shift focus for the sake of variety, matches the nonlinear way most people follow an interest over time, and gives them social capital by knowing something others are likely to value.

The Content Scoreboard can also help you monitor remedial work. If attitudes or relationships are at stake, plot also their learning of communication skills and life knowledge.

48. LANGUAGE AND MATH

The exactness inherent in language and math invites precise methods of instruction. Here we focus scoring to account for the gains made.

Accommodate Precision

Most processes in math and science involve formulas, definitions, and steps easily divided into points of knowledge. In languages, we can count as a point each vocabulary word or sentence translated, each grammar rule, and each verb or noun form. Many nouns and verbs have regular forms of declension or conjugation, so more points are not awarded for repeating forms unless they required more learning effort.

In both math and languages, single points of knowledge are often applied to diverse contexts, such as a math formula or a set of vocabulary or a grammar rule. Learning the point means mastering a representative sampling of its variant applications. We can refer to the quantity needed as a mastery count that brings a specific point of knowledge to the competence desired, the items needed in a set for students to comprehend its unifying principle.

In assigning pages of problems students learn uncertainly, however many they practice, they need at least a few they master perfectly. They might work a given number of problems with different data or note several instances generalizing an idea. Several dozen examples might suffice for a math process. Five uses of a foreign language word may round out its broader meaning. The applications that comprise the mastery count are each accorded a score as a valid point of knowledge. Babies seem able to learn the word for an object with three uses of it.

If your school's foreign language program is flexible, you can create your own expanding system to link associated meanings with appropriate variation. In putting words to foreign language sentences, award a point for each sentence that changes at least one word, up to a limit of five. In the sentence "I like to drink chocolate," change the word "chocolate" to "lemonade," "orange juice," "tea," and "coffee." Five alternate endings complete the main idea that you like to drink something. The term receives its maximum of five points.

Each sentence then can be altered in four other ways using the words associated with it. "I like to drink coffee" invites adjectives like "hot," "cold," "fresh," "strong." and verbs such as "drink," "pour," and "taste." A new adjective or verb inserted into a familiar sentence is a new point of knowledge. Three to five combinations usually provide the mind a sufficient base, although often-used words with many meanings may require a larger mastery count.

A single math principle usually incorporates knowledge from several angles. Even though the student may practice on a larger number, a teacher might require a student to complete a set of three problems to explain in detail. The score for the overall answer could include a point for each of the following: definition of terms such as area and trapezoid, purpose the principle is used for, assumptions involved in using it, formula given, steps of a problem-solving sequence, examples of problem solving with real numbers (up to three), part of a whole if the function is a portion of something else, and practical applications that might occur later. With such details synthesized, an answer to a math question might comprise a couple dozen points of knowledge.

The aim of such attention to detail, again, is a clear channel for effort leading to success. If you are not achieving your goals with your present methods, consider it.

49. READING

Sir Francis Bacon summed up the language skills students need: "Reading makes a full man, writing an exact man, and conference (conversation) a ready man." We want students full of valid knowledge but usually overhear banal conversations confined to a limited world.

Reading is the antidote, drawing students into the larger human condition and expanding their range of words and ideas. Some schools start the day with a "sacred" half-hour of reading nothing may interrupt. We might hope also for conscious learning from what they read. We want for them a refined internal model of human experience. We encourage this by arranging for them to express what they absorb.

We want an action set in their mind. When you say, "You're tutoring about this tomorrow," they expect to act. They think about the material differently, grasp it more deeply, and incorporate new ideas better. Similarly,

"You're going to do a stand-up report about this tomorrow," or "When you're done reading, explain to your partner what you read," or "Now tell the story."

Then, a tangible reason spurs them to lace pieces together thoughtfully. Unless they do this soon after they read, their later attempt is less coherent. Even exchanging brief comments about their reading has power beyond the minutes devoted to it, activating the social role of knowledge. We turn their reading into a vehicle for personal relationships.

To apply this, arrange them in pairs with each reading something different. Ask them to pause, say, every ten minutes and in a few sentences summarize to each other what they have read. If you allot 20% of their reading time for expressing it to a partner, you can end a fifty-minute reading period with "Tell your stories back and forth for five minutes each." Their reading gains social relevance when it connects them to another. They find they "have something going" with the other. Talking about their reading leads to being accepted and validated. They have an incentive to read well and tell in detail what they find.

Narrating knowledge as a story helps them integrate it. Assign them to find out who these people were who wrote this, and why they say these things. The sciences become more interesting this way, how someone met a challenge by pursuing an idea. Math concepts stick better incorporated into their history of events, personalities, and conditions. Story and background together nourish the imagination and are easier to draw on later. For variety, use Mental Movie between their reading and their narrating. Improve their exchange further with a half-minute for reviewing communication skills before and after.

A brief use of daily time is to write a question in their notebooks about what they read and a telegraphic answer to it. With even a minute a day at this they retain more. They can also talk later to a Designated Listener about their reading (cf. 33).

50. WRITING

As students build social capital by talking about what they read, they generate an Amazon of thought. We hone its expression as we develop their writing. First they need confidence in their word flow, that they can put words to their ideas. Then "Instead of speaking it today, write it down like you would say it." If this is too hard for primary students, let them dictate to a partner and then change roles.

After they can write a draft as a stream of thought, go then to mechanics, to guidelines that make their writing clear, efficient, and eventually elegant. Arrange for older students to give one on one encouragement if you can. The best inspiration for nearly any ability often comes from students slightly older.

From you they need individualized feedback. Each change you suggest is for them a new point of knowledge. Convey it as a positive point of learning rather than as a mistake, and credit them with a score as they can explain it back to you. Computerize the list of changes suggested to each student, and require them to apply the changes in future writing to maintain their score. With five corrections per paper, one paper a week, they accumulate 180 improvements in a school year. What drives their improvement is insisting they continue to use each correction once it is understood.

Often overlooked in the early grades is how kinesthetic children are, how much learning depends on their physical action with it. Learning letters, they must practice copying them, and then write by memory until they can do so rapidly. They claim new ideas by writing the words describing them, and readily own the tangible product of their effort.[33]

Chapter Eight

Demonstrate Learning

For confidence in their learning, students need to demonstrate it to each other, to parents, and to the educational system. Here we suggest how to report it and perform it.

51. ACADEMIC MASTERY REPORT

We assume here that the standard summative evaluations of students' learning are inadequate. They fail especially to inform anyone of what the student actually continues to know. We remedy this with a clear, easily certifiable criterion of mastered knowledge—the ability to explain something without help at any time—and sum it up subject by subject.

You can assemble the results of their learning practice in an individual Academic Mastery Report updated regularly. Record the total explaining time or number of points they achieve for each unit or section in every course and subject. Produce it weekly for special needs students and at least monthly for others. Demoralized students are encouraged by adding to their report at the end of every day. You might explain:

> Look at each section in your notebook. Find the questions you learned how to answer today, and list the number of points under each one that you can tell back. Add up all those points. Under Science, you remember, we dealt with worms and I put four points on the board. If you told back all four points, write Science: worms (4p). In math, we had fractions and covered eight points. If you got five of them by the end of the day, you could write Math: fractions (5p). In Literature, maybe you learned four lines of the poem and four other things we discussed about poetry, so write Literature: poetry (8p).

On subsequent days they add to totals in existing categories, and you start new ones. If they want to include personal interests, have a parent or student listen to them, score their explanation by time or points, and sign off on it.

They do the main accounting work. You teach the points you want retained, and they master them, count them, and record totals. You might also find a volunteer who will computerize their reports. Gather the week's data by Friday for processing over the weekend, and send them home or email them on Monday.

Because each digit represents a success, matches their effort perfectly, and describes learning they own and can demonstrate anytime, students are pleased to erase old scores, incorporate increases, show results to their parents, and maintain them. The report helps sustain their pride and continued effort. An example:

ACADEMIC MASTERY REPORT

Melissa Lewis

Audubon High School, 2015–2016

BIOLOGY: biology basics (59p), chemical compounds (16p), cells, DNA, life basics (85p), evolution (20p), classification and earth's beginnings (19p); bacteria, viruses (33p); algae, fungi, ferns (29p), seed plants (38p). Total 299 points.

RUSSIAN: declensions (85p), conjugations (70p), grammar rules (32p), vocabulary (933p), sentences (214p), dialogs (93 min). Total 1357 points, 1 hour 33 minutes.

MATH: definitions of terms (93p), rules (23p), demonstration problems (150p), problem-solving steps (545p), applications (87p). Total 898 points.

U.S. HISTORY: events and characteristics (163p), names and terms in military conflicts (79p), important people (51p); political, social, and cultural terms (41p), historical narrative 1600–1850 (27:10), Civil War era 1850–1865 (33:22), rebuilding South 1865–1900 (12:35), industry and expansion to 1900 (24:13), politics and protest to 1900 (15:51), Progressive Movement to 1920 (19:17), World War I (20:19), Depression and New Deal (9:23). Total 334 points, 2 hours 42 minutes 10 seconds.

GEOGRAPHY: place names (131p), terms (88p), maps (37p), earth surface (39p), climate/vegetation (47p), population (29p), culture (32p), North America (27p), Latin America (31p), Europe (67p), Russia and eastern Europe (11p), Africa and SW Asia (14p), SE Asia (8p), Australia and polar (36p). Total 378 points.

WRITING: corrected errors (38p), principles of composition (29p), grammar rules (19p), personal journal (2,555 words), field logbook (667 words), reports for classes (1,116 words), first draft writing (1,982 words), edited writing (3,825 words), poetry (175 words). Total 86 points, and 10,320 words written.

ACADEMIC MASTERY REPORT

TOTALS. Points: 299, 1357, 898, 334, 378, 86 = 3,352 points. Time: 2 hours 42 minutes 10 seconds. Writing: 10,320 words.

CERTIFICATION: this is to certify that we, John Smith and Adam Smith, questioned this student for (length of time) two hours on (date) June 16, 2016, drawing questions randomly from the original records of the summary above. Our finding is that this student knew (percent) 98% of the knowledge claimed.

DATE: June 17, 2007 SIGNED John Smith SIGNED Adam Smith

---

52. PUBLIC PERFORMANCES

A topic performance is a formal public speaking event when students present one or more Learning Feats. It becomes more significant as the audience expands. Arrange for a room to accommodate student performers and their guests. If your options are a space larger than you need or one with a tight fit, go with the smaller. A crowded room increases emotional impact.

Limit their offerings to a length all can perform in an evening presentation. Print a program listing each one's topic, time, and room number, and give them a supply to distribute to their relatives and neighbors. Everyone they invite increases their motivation to prepare. Get students working quietly, call parents on the phone, and compliment their child's preparation for the event.

On the assigned day, students and parents go to their designated rooms. Students are called on as scheduled, rise to give their performance, accept applause, acknowledge it till it dies down, and return to their seats. A brief award ritual dignifies their achievement and boosts pride. A certificate might contain the student's name, the date, and a description of their feat such as "Described ten animals found on Mount Kilimanjaro," or "Explained the historical development of geometry," or "Described how to clean a fish."

Provide refreshments and a socializing time. At home, parents can fix the certificate to the wall and say, "We were there when you did that."

A curriculum performance draws on everything learned to date. One way is with "top twenty," a set of inclusive questions larger than the number of students in the class that incorporate the entire curriculum. The questions need not be the same for everyone. Each can alternatively write out their personal list of major performable questions to give you.

Place counters in a bag up to the agreed-on number of questions. Draw names randomly, and as students advance to the front of the room, a member of the audience (perhaps one of their guests) draws a counter. You look at the student's list and ask the question corresponding to that number (or any next in sequence that has not already been asked), creating a game-like atmosphere with an element of chance. The student answers one or more questions on the topic up to the time allotted.

In this design students essentially prepare twenty or more talks to give instead of a single one. Few or none answer the same question, so differences in ability are muted. Each receives celebration, and the emotional dynamic is the same for all.

An alternate design is to have students write on separate slips every individual question they can answer and place them in an individual bag. They can accumulate a substantial fund of these by adding a few every day that they practice with partners and in Impromptu Performances. At the public event, someone draws a slip from their bag and asks the question written on it, skipping those asked already. The student speaks for the time allotted. One answer might take twenty-five seconds, another answer two minutes, and a third a minute and a half.

Award certificates can acknowledge students' entire Learning Feat total from which selection is made instead of the few they perform. Eight minutes performing may validate ninety-two minutes of learning just as a few test questions stand in for ten times as many not asked. Their certificate might read, "Demonstrated mastery of ninety-two minutes of Learning Feats from five subjects." With their award certificate, each has a description of their feat read aloud and applause.

53. CHECKPOINT MORNING

To guarantee learning, engage students in a mastery-producing task until they produce mastery. Occasional use of Checkpoint Morning can stimulate students from upper elementary on. It spurs selecting, organizing, recording, mastering, and performing learning. Students enjoy freedom while teachers control results. Students show they can explain knowledge without help for a measured time.

Find a room rich in resources such as a library, a kitchen timer or a clock with a visible second hand, and a list of the students with space by their names for recording their accomplishment. Say to them:

> You're going to have an interesting experience this morning. From any of your texts or other sources in the room, I want you to find something of interest to learn (specify subject matter as you wish). When you have a minute's worth of learning from it, you'll teach it to someone else. As you read, think, "How would I explain this?" When your explanation runs at least a minute, arrange it as question and answer. Write out at the top of your notes the question or

> questions you have chosen and your answer below. What you can say in a minute is about a page of writing, so aim for that and then time it. When you have your questions and answers written, trade yours with someone else. You each copy the other's, and then together learn both your own and the other person's. Explain them back and forth to each other until you both know both answers. When you and your partner have learned at least two minutes' worth, come to me and let me hear it. Show me your written record and be able to talk for two minutes without repeating yourself. When you have done that, you will be free to go to the activity we agreed on.

Guide the experience firmly and insist on results. If your class already sets to work at what you ask of them, they may not need a reward activity afterward, but you might wish to provide one anyway. If many underperform, unhappy feelings divide them, or they lack discipline and concentration, a reward can jump-start them into cooperating. Ideally it should be something they can turn to right away when they complete the task or a more valued one toward which they can accumulate points.

Reward options might be use of school computers, audiovisual or exercise equipment, or watching a video. They might play quiet games one to one or go to a gym or playground. Consider also a reward that totals up points as a group: "When we get a hundred minutes of mastered learning from everyone together, we'll have a game-hour instead of class." Discuss options that appeal to them.

Help those needing assistance to find a topic. They read for ten to thirty minutes, write down a question and its extended answer, and then find someone else. They sit together, trade papers, copy down what the other gathered, ask questions to understand it, and practice explaining both papers back and forth. When they feel ready to face your checking, they approach you and demonstrate their knowledge. Having their notes in front of you, you need not hear the whole two minutes, but can spot-check details. A few work intensively for thirty minutes so they can begin the reward activity. Everyone goes at their own pace and you monitor and aid as needed. In doing these things, they

Survey their own interests.
Practice research skills.
Talk about ideas.
Organize them as question and answer.
Summarize them in writing.
Relate to another student.
Exchange learning.
Install knowledge in short-term memory.
Exert self-discipline.
Follow directions.

Initiate a system for accumulating learning.

Not bad for a nearly free morning. Everyone succeeds and feels connected to someone else. You can assure learning because you can send them back for more work if they are short of the two minutes, if they goofed off and must keep working while their friends receive the reward activity. If some do not produce the two minutes, you essentially make them a deal. Since they failed to use "freedom leading to results," you switch to "control leading to results." The next day they sit beside you and work under your supervision.

On subsequent days, you can ask them first to retain the prior day's ideas and work on specific subjects: "By the end of the week, learn something from math, American literature, and science." They work at their own pace and expand their knowledge. You consult with them on subject matter and monitor the activity.

54. PRACTICE MAKES PERMANENT TEAM COMPETITIONS

Group competition energizes almost any activity, but schools usually neutralize its benefits by advancing winners and excluding the less skilled who need the team experience most. The design here includes everyone, and draws on scoring with points of knowledge as explained previously. Three stages offer different levels of challenge.

Stage One

The beginning stage is carried out in a single classroom. Small teams master knowledge in a short time and submit to questioning by an opposing team.

1. Object of the competition. Students work together in small groups to learn all they can in three to five days. You can specify a subject or let them add to all their courses. Their effort in preparing is the main benefit of the competition, stimulated by the prospect of accounting for it to each other.
2. Participants. To make teams balanced in ability, list each student's current total of scored learning to date. Combine them to make initial team totals as equal as possible while spreading out class leaders. You might consult students' suggestions for composing teams (cf. also 18. Organization Groups). An even number of teams makes competition easier. Even numbers on each team also aids their practice sessions though most classes involve a mix of team sizes.

Different ability levels may have separate leagues (think Special Olympics) but within a given grade, team composition should even out different abilities. Three bright students might help one less accomplished in a great experience for all. Point out that team totals are equal at the start.

3. Concentration Time. After identifying teams, plan several days of "Concentration Time" preparing. Each team works together either to expand their answers on any questions they already learned or add new ones. They locate and organize new information in clear notes in the content you assign, teach it to each other, and share their notes for others to photocopy or write out. When they add to existing notes, they mark where the new competition material begins.
4. The Exchange. A half-hour before match time, opposing teams exchange copies of the questions team members claim to answer, the new material gathered and learned during Concentration Time. Teams examine their opponents' lists to decide what questions they want to ask of individuals on the other team. The judge appointed for the meet—preferably a teacher or older student familiar with students' knowledge—determines that the learning is valid for their grade level.
5. The Meet. Matches between teams can be drawn randomly on meet day. Schedule them into different rooms of the school before their own judge, parents, and visitors. Two ways of judging teams that have different numbers of members are (a) for the judge to weigh the average per-student knowledge gained on each team or (b) for the larger team to sideline one or more members by drawing straws.

Before each round, place the names of its members in a team cup, and from one team draw a point student who answers questions, and from the other team a questioner. The point student gives his or her answer material to the judge.

All questions addressed to the point student go through the questioner. Others on the questioning team may help by passing notes, whispering, or pointing to questions to ask next. The same length of questioning time for everyone is set by the teacher—between three and six minutes. Questioning probes any weaknesses in the point student's claimed knowledge. Once the questioner feels she has uncovered the strength of an answer, she can interrupt the point student by saying "Thank you" and asking a different question.

The judge weighs the total knowledge the student claims to have gained during Concentration Time by how well he or she responds to the specific questions asked, and assigns an overall percent score, affirming how much of what was asked was known. Five minutes of competent answers might validate fifty minutes of learning claimed.

When the first questioning is completed, the direction of it switches. A point student's name is drawn from the other team, and a questioner from the team that just answered. The participants from the immediately preceding round are given a rest unless they are the last on their team to fill the role.

6. Final Score. When all students have been questioned, the judge decides which team obtained the most new mastered answers during Concentration Time, and names the winner. For a more exact score, the judge can (a) total together all the points of knowledge each student on the team claims to have added during Concentration Time and (b) multiply that number of points by the average percent that students on that team demonstrated they knew during the questioning.

   Thus if the judge rates two students at 90% and two at 80%, the team's rating is 85%. The total knowledge all the team members claim to have mastered and is then multiplied by 85% and the highest resulting team score wins. (For comparison, see Appendix 10, the Individual Match Worksheet used with Stage Three, but here without the calculation for each separate question).
7. Next Meet. The same team compositions continue in succeeding meets if their skills in the first are comparable enough that outcomes are uncertain and winning depends on their effort. If teams are clearly uneven, assign new ones unless they are so cohesive that all would rather stay together. If you have any doubt, ask for anonymous written feedback.

Stage Two

This expands the prior design. The meet and the manner of scoring are the same except:

1. Teams may be from more than one classroom or school.
2. Concentration Time is not used.
3. All learning is welcome including personal interests, hobbies, books read, special areas of expertise, prior or additional work for any course, and the entire year's curriculum to date. Students need only separate their material into question and answer, score it by time or points, and organize it in writing well enough that a judge can follow it.
4. Because of the larger quantity of learning involved, the time between the exchange and the meet is longer, allowing perhaps an hour or more for teams to prepare the questions they will ask of their opponents.

5. The judge declares which team demonstrates the largest quantity of learning overall. If teams have an unequal number of members, they are compared on the basis of average per-student score (total learning divided by the number of students on the team) after the calculation explained in point 6 above.

Stage Three

In Stage Three, scores are determined as accurately as possible, and the meet outcome depends partly on how teams use skill and judgment during the meet. The design accommodates interschool competition involving numerous teams and two or more upper elementary, middle, or high schools. The teams submit to each other the Learning Feats they have mastered, challenge each other's claimed knowledge, scoring shifts back and forth as questions validate or find weakness in a score claimed, and winners are determined. Comprehensive material can be included, and judging is more precise.

Specific terms refer to features of the competition. Students prepare by developing a clear question and answer summary of everything they know, team members help each other expand their knowledge, and they assign a score of points or time for each answer. Answer lengths are sectioned to include learning of any quantity.

At the meet, competing teams exchange a complete list of the questions their members can answer. Students question each other in one-on-one matches while a judge rates the point student question by question. A scoring team converts the judge's ratings to team scores, and points taken from one team during the meet are awarded to the other. Changes in score are posted as the match proceeds, and the team ending with the highest point total is the winner.

Here we outline the guidelines of the competition and explain each in detail:

Remote Preparation

1. The Focus
2. Team Makeup
3. Team Practices

Learning Format

4. Individual Learning Feat (ILF) List
5. Total Team Challenge (TTC)
6. Long Answers
7. Short Answers
8. The Five-Second Rule

Final Preparation

9. The Checkout
10. The Exchange
11. The Strategy Session
12. Risk/Reward

The Meet

13. The Setting
14. The Questioning
15. Completeness Criteria

Judging

16. Judges
17. Scoring
18. Outcomes
19. Interschool Meets

Individual Match Worksheet

Remote Preparation

1. The Focus. A focus for the meet can deepen study and generate conversation among team members. Organizers might open it to all knowledge or confine it to a subject like math, science, or history and incorporate both curricular and personal interest material; scientific or nature-related programs on video or television; and regional, ethnic, and cultural matters. Issues of public concern, economics, and world conditions may be timely. If no focus is set, all knowledge meeting the criteria below is eligible.
2. Team Makeup. Competing classrooms or schools divide entire classes into teams of equal ability, each a representative mix of the students of that grade level (cf. Stage One, 2. Participants). Using an even number (four or six if possible) makes pairing easier during team practices.
3. Team Practices. Hour-long practice sessions can be scheduled before, during (e.g. at lunch), or after the class day. Team members prepare to recall and explain everything they know, organizing and mastering all schoolwork well enough to relate it readily to a questioner. Middle and high schools could make Learning Competition a separate course for mastering other courses. In the practices, team members (a) bring information they have collected and made notes on, (b) add each other's material to their own, (c) write out answers they develop together,

(d) help each other understand and explain all the learning they collect, (e) invent strategies for remembering it more easily, and (f) verify and sign off on each other's times and points.

Learning Format

4. Individual Learning Feat (ILF) List. A Learning Feat is a chunk of learning arranged as a question and answer, and timed (or points of knowledge counted) by a listening partner. Team practices result in increases to students' ILF lists. Times of prior feats are lengthened or new ones are added. The length of the answering time (or the number of new points of knowledge) attained is noted under each question beside the initials of the person checking it. Examples:

   Describe the ten largest rivers in the world. 9:45t JE = 9 minutes 45 seconds of time verified by student J. E.
   Explain five principles of geometry. 5:13t LS = 5 minutes 13 seconds of time verified by student L. S.
   Compare politics before the American Revolution with today's. 6:00t FM, 11:16t CS = 6 minutes time verified first by student F. M. and later 11 minutes 16 seconds by student C. S.
   Explain the plot of Great Expectations. 15:30 FM = 15 minutes 30 seconds by F. M.
   Give five Spanish words used in the kitchen and their English meaning. 5p KL = 5 points verified by student with initials K. L.
   Define trapezoid and how to obtain its area. 5p HT, 8p KL
   Explain five ways students gain good feelings in school. 5p LS
   Name four stages in the life cycle of a large aquatic mammal. 4p PP

The answers to some of the questions are specified in points and can be used as they are. Others with a lengthy timed answer can be broken into increments during questioning. The ten largest rivers divide reasonably into comments about each or can be chunked by continent. A questioner might ask first, "What are the names of the ten largest rivers?" and follow up with "Please tell all you know about the Nile." Five principles in geometry are similarly separable. The question about American politics invites arbitrary division before the competition (cf. 6 below), perhaps by issues, people, motivations, cause and effect, events, or time lines. The contents of a novel might be segmented by beginning, middle, and end; or by events, themes, and characters.

5. Total Team Challenge (TTC). The times and points of each participant's Learning Feats are totaled to obtain their ILF score. The ILF scores of all team members added together are the TTC, a list of the questions everyone can answer and the time or point scores of each. Parts of ILF lists are likely to be the same, and others individualized. Progress in practices increases the TTC the team can defend in the upcoming match.
6. Long Answers. The length of an answer affects both integration of the knowledge and the pace of questioning, values that conflict. The competition is most spirited with answers that are brief and checkable, but we also want to build academic mastery with answers as long as possible, even to explaining an entire subject. To combine both goals, divide answers longer than three minutes (the equivalent of twelve points) into two or more smaller answers. A student with an eight-minute answer might say "I'm going to answer in three parts." He or she names the parts, each of which becomes its own question if the questioner asks for it. A twenty-minute question might have three or four major parts chunked further into portions under three minutes.

   Accurate scoring depends on knowing the length of a claimed answer. The list given to the opposing team includes all the questions that have answers three minutes or less so each team can reasonably estimate what the other knows.
7. Short Answers. While typically we ask students to express their answers in complete sentences, an exception could be straight memory material that organizers agree could have answers of a single word, phrase, or data bit. Even small pieces that took independent effort to learn deserve a point of score. Examples are spellings, times tables, formulas, definitions, and subject-related vocabulary. For foreign language vocabulary, organizers can agree on the direction of translation. Early in the year they might work on passive understanding—the term in the foreign language and the answer translating it into English (What does *comer* mean?).

   Later when students have enlarged their passive vocabulary, reverse the direction with the term in English and the translation in the foreign language (How do you say "to eat" in Spanish?). Organizers can compile lists of scientific and mathematical terms to include or accept glossary definitions as legitimate brief answers (cf. point 10 below).

   To collapse points and time into a single measure, convert them at the rate of four points to one minute (cf. 46. Score by Points and Time for more on this). With these guidelines, long and short answers and both points and time can be included in the same overall score.

8. The Five-Second Rule. A superficial way to learn is to chop everything into answers as brief as possible. The five-second rule accounts for the information supplied by a question that makes answering easier, and benefits the team that converts its questions instead into the most comprehensive arrangement. The rule treats as just one question any question that a student can outline into chunks and the chunks into pieces that he or she can go into at any level asked. This encourages students to expand their chunk size and avoid multiple individual smaller questions that cost them a five-second time.

   To apply the rule, count the total number of questions on the ILF lists of a team's members for which students can outline the answers completely. Multiply that number by five seconds, and subtract the product from the team's TTC. One team member may have 60 questions with multiple parts to each (60 × 5 seconds = 300 seconds or 5 minutes deducted), while another may have comparable overall learning but four times as many brief questions (240 questions × 5 seconds each = 20 minutes). A third may be able to outline his or her entire ILF list, waiving the five-second rule.

   At the Checkout (below), each student marks the question sets he or she can tell back from one question. A single question "packages" visibly all the information in sub-questions that a student claims to know. This information is available to the judge and to the opposing team at the Exchange and can be challenged during questioning.

Final Preparation

9. The Checkout. The last practice session before the meet is "the checkout." Students score ILFs they have not scored already, add up their collective ILF scores to produce the TTC, assemble in a package all the papers containing their questions that have claimed scores no longer than three minutes but without the answer details, and make a copy of it for the opposing team and judge.
10. The Exchange. For the first meet, teams exchange lists an hour ahead and decide afterward if they want more time or less for future meets. An issue to settle is that each team accept the other's TTC as valid learning. To pad their record, a team might go to a dictionary and pick out a thousand common words they already know how to spell and claim an extra thousand points apiece for each member.

    Teams need to agree instead that the opposing team's material is valid for their grade level. If it is not, they protest it to their teacher who either works it out with the opposing team or present the issue to the judge for resolution (possibly adjusting the TTC lower) before the competition begins. Organizers avoid such problems by agreeing ahead about acceptable categories of knowledge. A second issue is that questions exchanged must be legible and neat so they do not inhibit questioning.

11. The Strategy Session. In the time between the Exchange and the Meet, with the opposing team's valid TTC in hand, team members study it to select the Learning Feats on it they believe give them the best edge in questioning; where opponents may be vulnerable and their own knowledge can help them expose it. They also might wish to scramble after sources on unfamiliar ideas. They prepare a list of questions for each opponent that anyone on their own team can use when named questioner.

    They might also note from the opposing team's list that they can expect intense questioning themselves on specific subjects and decide to refresh their knowledge about them. Teams may need less than an hour to do this, so the meet can begin anytime both teams are ready.

12. Risk/Reward. The beginning TTC is the basis of the team's score. The scoring system rewards the team that risks the most, that declares the maximum knowledge they think they can defend. The higher the initial TTC, the better the chance of winning. Yet including shaky knowledge invites the other team to expose it and gain points for itself. If the TTC scores are close at the start of the meet, the team prepared to challenge the opposing team with probing questions and defend its own answers does the best. The possibility that any Learning Feat may be challenged is a motive for mastering each one.

The Meet

13. The Setting. Places are arranged for the two students who will exchange questions and answers. They face each other at opposite ends of a long table or at small tables several feet apart, far enough that teams can whisper without being heard by the other team. The judge sits to the side midway between the two teams, receives lists of the team members with two columns beside their names headed "Point Student" and "Questioner," and checks them off as they fill these roles.

14. The Questioning. A coin toss determines which team answers first. The judge randomly draws the name of the point student (Joe), and the questioner (Sharon). Joe hands his questions and answers to the judge. The judge or scoring team keeps time with an automatic timer that beeps when time is up. The questioning turn is five minutes for six-person teams, six minutes for four-person teams, or of a length agreed on by the organizers (who may modify any rule they wish). Sharon asks questions that challenge the knowledge Joe claimed on his ILF

list. Others on her team can relay questions to her verbally or in writing to ask Joe but she, as the assigned questioner, determines which to ask. This guideline aids the team whose members have thoroughly shared everything they know beforehand instead of relying on a few expert members. Also, a team pausing to reconsider strategy loses time for challenging the point student.

Sharon continues to question Joe for the time allotted on any legitimate part of a Learning Feat he claims to know. If his ILF list cites minutes of knowledge about the Bill of Rights, he should be able to describe what the First Amendment can mean for a citizen. Joe may answer correctly, be wrong, be vague and unclear, repeat himself, or show insightful understanding. He answers to the limit of his five- or six-minute time while the judge consults his answer pages to verify that his answers fit the knowledge he claims. If Joe regards a question as beyond his claimed knowledge, he can answer, "That isn't on my list." If the questioner disagrees about this, the issue is left to the judge along with the student's overall performance.

Sharon can end any of Joe's answers by saying "Thank you" when she thinks he has revealed the extent of his knowledge, and ask another question. If she and her team suspect that he cannot answer for a score he claims, they can make a tactical decision to ask him to tell all of that answer or may presume that the judge notices the lack and try to find other weak knowledge. Joe can answer, "I don't know that," and hope that with the next question he can demonstrate more mastery.

A team questioned may realize that they have just given answers they had planned to ask the other team, making it easier for the other team to respond. Their competence shows up as they shift quickly to a different tack. Questioning switches from one team to the other. The judge draws the next point student and questioner and allows the two who just competed to rest for a turn unless they are the last from their team.

15. Completeness Criteria. The following criteria can help a judge decide whether to take points from the answering team and award them to the questioning team:

- Fluency. If the point student talks at less than a normal rate of speed, subtract the percent of slowness compared to normal talking speed.

- Padding. Does the student supply information appropriate for a lower grade that entailed no learning effort? Direct experience should be combined with academic learning. A question on geology is not answered adequately by narrating a vacation in a national park ("The mountains were really big . . . .")
- Repetition. Occasional restatement is normal, but for a pattern of repetition, subtract the proportion of repeated time from the student's total score.
- Deficit. Was something omitted that reasonably should have been in the claimed answer? Check for obvious gaps in the outline submitted and the answer given.
- Inaccuracy. Was something declared true that isn't?
- Illogicality. Did the point student connect ideas inappropriately, revealing a lack of understanding?
- Integration. Judges can award extra points to balance off those lost (or even increase an ILF score) as students link ideas flexibly and insightfully, add more knowledge than claimed, and synthesize information. Aggressive questioning usually reveals the degree of integration achieved.

Judging

16. Judges. Judges' fairness in crediting individuals' knowledge, applying their standard consistently to everyone, is essential to a good competition. They do so by comparing a student's actual answer to his or her claimed answer for each question and assigning it a percentage. If stage fright disables students from taking their turn, organizers can agree on a second chance after others are questioned.

    Judges may be anyone from the school or community but preferably people familiar with students' foundation of knowledge. Older students might help. More than one judge may be used and their tallies averaged. Do not schedule parents to judge their own children because other participants will question their objectivity.

    Judges can meet ahead to learn the process and scoring. They assume a role similar to that of a referee in a sports contest to settle disagreements about rules that have not already been resolved by organizers.
17. Scoring. Judges use the Individual Match Worksheet to score each student independently. Immediately after each question and answer, judges assign a percent of validity to it, a conclusion about Joe's mastery using the seven criteria above, focusing just on what they hear that demonstrates learning on the ILF items questioned.

The overall proportion of mastery of the questions answered is applied later to the student's total score. If the judge awards 90% validity to Joe's knowledge on the items questioned, 10% of his total score claimed is transferred to the other team. If Joe began with an ILF score of 2,000 points, 200 points are awarded to the other team and Joe's score is reduced to 1800. If his team's TTC posted on the scoreboard at the start was 10,000, it is reduced on the scoreboard to 9,800 and the opposing team's TTC is increased by 200 points.

Judges can award the other team as much of Joe's score as they deem fair: 1%, 10%, or even 100% if Joe knows nothing that he claimed to know. If the point student responds perfectly on the questions asked (which may be a twentieth of his list), 100% credit is given for his total claimed score.

A scoring team can speed the scoring process. After entering a percent of validity for each separate question, the judge hands the worksheet to the scoring team that completes the calculations on it during the next round. So as not to distract questioning, it posts the results on the scoreboard between rounds, maintaining a running tally of each team's total. Scores (changing the TTC up or down) occur when a point student has less than or more than the complete knowledge about the question he or she claimed to know (cf. Individual Match Worksheet, Appendix 10, for detailed instructions).

18. Outcomes. The winning team has the highest team score after all questioning and judging are completed and points exchanged.

    Between meets, students might plot their team accomplishments on separate line charts (dates across the top and the scores up the side) for the following values:

- Initial TTC going into each meet.
- Meet Scores, the team's total score after changes from the questioning are included. If this line is above or below the prior one, you might discuss the solidity of the learning they claim, or congratulate them on their skill in questioning opposing teams.
- Improvement. This is the difference between a team's scores that concluded the previous and current meets. The team with the biggest gain from one to the next wins the Improvement Contest. Even if they don't win the meet, scoring well on the Improvement Contest boosts a team's self-image.
- Win/Loss Championship. This counts wins and losses for all meets during a season. The team with the most wins by the end of the season is the school champion.

- High Score Championship. The team that knows the most at the end of the season has the high score, determined by the highest of the final TTCs of all the teams in one school or grade (after points are subtracted in the competition). A team that starts slowly can accelerate through the year and still become school champion by this measure.

19. Interschool Meets. Bringing entire grades from one school to another for a meet might be logistically daunting. To include everyone in the energy of the meet, begin with an intramural league in each school that incorporates everyone on sixty teams, for example. For a trip to another school that can accommodate eighteen teams, all sixty prepare, expecting to represent the school. The day before the meet, the eighteen participating are drawn.

    At the meet site, match teams either by random draw, or schools with prior intraschool leagues and records of team wins and losses can bring together their ranked teams if they prefer: top against top, second against second, and so on. If one school arrives with fewer teams than the other, the larger school draws a random number equal to the smaller school's.

    The winning school of the meet is determined by the number of its competing teams winning. With eighteen teams from each school, one with ten or more winners is the Meet Champion. With equal numbers of winning teams, judges can declare a draw or break the tie by calculating the sum of the total final scores of the competing teams.

    Schools can compete in overall school learning (whether teams went to the meet or not) by two measures. One is the All-School Combined Score (ACS) for schools of similar size. This compares the total scores of all of both schools' teams. To calculate this, competing teams obtain their final verified TTC without adding to it the competition points they might gain from the other team. If they lose points during the match (making their verified TTC lower than their initial), the average percentage of that loss among all their competing teams is applied to all their noncompeting teams also.

    Competing teams together losing five percent by judges' ratings lower the scores of the noncompeting teams also by that percent. When these adjustments are made to a school's team scores, the total of all of them represents an adjusted TTC for that school, called the All-School Combined Score (ACS). Between schools, the winner has the higher adjusted TTC total. A harder working smaller school can readily outscore a larger one.

A second measure equalizes size differences and compares their learning achievement fairly regardless of how many students attend each school. The All-School Combined Score (ACS) is divided by the number of students enrolled in the school or participating grade to obtain the average student TTC score, which is called the "All-School Individual Score" (AIS). In both of these measures, every student's score matters, so students are likely to say, "We want to win the all-school titles. Come on, let's help you!"

Chapter Nine

Implementation

Accumulating knowledge requires unremitting will to counteract the human propensity to distraction and lethargy. We try to accustom students to channel their unfocused energy into lifetime learning.

The means arises from the nature of reality: Organize the lower so the higher can flow freely. The higher is the universe of knowledge. The lower are the physical behaviors of reading, speaking, listening, writing, and recalling ideas. Organizing the lower admits us to the higher.

EVALUATING THE APPROACH

Before introducing new methods, consider gathering baseline data so you can say later, "Here's where we came from." Students are encouraged when they see measured progress, your own effort is reinforced, and others have something to judge by.

Measure students' knowledge first. The design is aimed at increasing what they not only remember but can call up at will, so we focus on that kind. Obtain a baseline by asking students, without warning or aid, to write down all they know about the subject(s) you teach. They then exchange papers and go through them with you. You explain what represents a valid score in their answers, clarify any uncertainties, and credit them with all their points of knowledge—the details, terms, steps, examples, and separable pieces of overview and structure that comprise points as explained in our design. Determine an individual total for each one.

Use the methods given here for a month or more, test again without warning, and compare results. The quantity of their remembered learning will probably jump by 30% in even a month. They should remember everything they knew on the first test and almost everything they practiced after it.

You may also wish to administer standardized tests before it and after the program has operated for a year. The intervening time needs to be longer because tests are less likely designed to tap what your students explicitly master.

Even slow accumulation of learning shows impressive power. Imagine a student taking a full fifteen minutes just to learn one worthy idea contained in a single sentence. He grasps something new, gives it form, and saves it—a new idea every fifteen minutes, four per hour. At this pace five hours a day, in a week he has 100 ideas, in thirty-six weeks 3,600 ideas, and in twelve years 43,200 ideas.

Speed is not decisive. Even at turtle pace half that fast—two ideas per hour—in twelve years he has 21,600 ideas. The critical point is saving instead of forgetting. To be wildly successful, he need only retain ideas steadily, which is easy if he does not permit his learning to evaporate.

Besides increasing learning, the design also alters attitudes. To assess such changes unobtrusively, arrange for staff to log in raw data: library checkouts showing interest in learning, changes in litter and graffiti revealing respect for property (with countable measures like cleanup hours or number of pieces of litter picked up), in-class disciplinary events, referrals to principal, suspensions, unsolicited parental praise, absences and tardiness for all reasons, illnesses reported to school nurse, thefts, return of lost items, reports of violence and their degree of severity, conversations solicited with staff, students choosing to continue class work outside class, and numbers of students identifying others as friendly or helpful.

Collect baseline data for a week or more before beginning the new design; then either continue collecting it to monitor progress, or resume the measures several months later.

DIRECT EFFORT

How you direct their effort is crucial. Enormous potential energy lies before us to arouse and organize, filling each moment with an activity of value. Time matters, and we use it purposefully.

Students welcome being mobilized and can be stimulated by intensive discipline—seen usually in the gymnasium instead of the classroom. An instructive incident about this occurred while I was in college. During my turn as lieutenant in the Reserve Officers Training Corps, the Corps participated in a public event on the football field. My platoon and I were standing in formation on a side street beforehand and time was passing slowly.

"Hey Lieutenant, how about some close order drill?" someone called out.

I brightened, sang out "Atten-HUT!" and the platoon came to attention. For several minutes within the confines of a single street and cadets on either side of us watching, I called out commands that they followed one after another: "Forward, march. To the rear, march. By the right flank, march," and so on. Everyone knew what to do. When we returned to our assigned spot, they felt refreshed, and the remaining time passed quickly.

The typical K–12 period may engage their energy little—for perhaps 10–15 minutes—with the rest open to distraction or boredom. What teachers do most of—talking and presenting—is for students passive time, asking little effort of them. They know you are sure to repeat anything they do not grasp the first time, that you will reexplain repeatedly.

Instead, take as little of the class hour for your part as possible. The Army's use of time in conveying a skill to recruits in past years was 5% of it explaining, 10% demonstrating, and 85% practicing. These ratios applied to a fifty-minute period would mean seven minutes conveying knowledge and students practicing it for forty-three minutes. Be efficient as you present material to save maximum time for their effort. When you lead the class for a sustained time, pause frequently for a minute or two so they can explain the material to each other or check their ongoing Peg List (cf. 31) to preserve key ideas.

THE DECISION TO WRITE

An important decision that makes possible the gains we describe is your choice about hard copy, whether or not you insist that they write out answers and summaries of the material. Some considerations:

1. When you write out concise answers on the board for them, they grasp what is important, increase their concentration, and gain a learning tool. When they are able to assemble answers independently, you can cease writing them out, but if some cannot do this, your help in writing may determine their learning.
2. Writing it yourself paces you while steering their effort. You declare your priorities by deciding, "This point is worth writing out so they get it." If it is not important enough to you to write it out, why is it worth their sustained labor to master it? Expecting them to learn more than you or they are willing to write out invites asking "How much of this will stick?"

3. Writing the answers aligns you with their rhythms of absorbing knowledge, shifting you from an attitude of "I hope most of you get this" to "I'm writing this down because I expect everyone to get it."
4. Writing is decisive for many students because it focuses them on a specific answer they can practice for 100% mastery. Ask them to print their notes for legibility, shareability, and speed. The physical effort to create tidy, readable notes channels attention—important especially for the less focused. As they write, walk around and look over their shoulders. Make sure everyone records question, answer, and score in the appropriate places.

KEY CHOICES

Implementing the preceding design boils down to a choice of whether or not to do a few things differently from your usual. Note four important issues and the sections where they are treated:

1. Will you organize their notebooks to make it easy for them to accumulate new material in a form they can easily practice to mastery (section 1)?
2. Will you make sure everyone understands the material the first time you present it (section 2)?
3. Will you generate or provide thorough hard copy of everything you want them to retain permanently, expressed in question and answer form for easy practice? (sections 3–4)?
4. Will you arrange the time for them to practice expressing and explaining their learning so that everyone steadily masters and retains everything you present (sections 5–6)?

While the approach offers many ways to retain and assimilate learning and develop social-emotional skills, these four decisions define whether or not you are teaching for retained learning or are content with familiarized learning.

GROUP CHANGE STRATEGY

In designing formats for your students, include (1) a few clear, observable guidelines, (2) a specific time in which to apply them, (3) accurate determination of results, and (4) recognition for success.

If your school's staff decides to undertake a change process, helpful points are (1) that it affects people strongly when they believe they can make a real difference, and (2) its importance (such as the impact on students' lives and how their success could help others) guides how much energy they will put in. (3) The change should have a clear definition, specific objectives, and time frame. (4) People are more motivated when they account to each other, so arrange reports back to the group. (5) They learn by reflecting on what enables the group to succeed or causes it to fail. (6) As they appreciate each other and feel their contributions valued, they will take more risks, and change to the extent that the group helps them think through the meaning of the experience for their lives and work. (7) Leaders' personal sacrifice and commitment give emotional meaning to everyone's efforts.[34] People said of one effective principal, "He went around blotting up spilled feelings so no one would slip on them."

TEACHER CHECKLIST

Any half-dozen of the following practices cause improvement, but for dramatic results in a couple weeks, do them all:

Classroom Order and Cooperation

1. Do I help students organize their learning tools?
2. Do I maintain order with appropriate consequences?
3. Do I exert personal influence to obtain cooperation?

Presentation

4. Do I create interesting classes manifesting reality, truth, love, and wisdom?
5. Do I define priorities I want students to master hour by hour?
6. Do I put key knowledge in question and answer form?
7. Do I pace new material to their assimilation of prior material?

Mastery

8. Do I schedule enough practice for them to obtain new mastery daily?
9. Do I provide daily mental recall?
10. Do I space follow-up practice to insure long-term retention?

Scoring

11. Do I monitor students' accurate scoring of each other's mastered work?

12. Do I post their daily increment of new mastery?
13. Do I provide each a periodic Academic Mastery Report?

Good Feelings

14. Do I teach them how to manage their feelings?
15. Do I arrange for them to give each other good feelings?
16. Do the students and I master good communication skills?

Performances

17. Do I arrange performances of learning?
18. Do they share their learning with a designated listener?

Besides teachers, others can initiate features of the design. Parents can sponsor performances, organize Designated Listeners, listen daily to everything their children can explain without help, and encourage teachers to teach for mastery. Advisors of student organizations and coaches can use Appreciation Time, the vocabulary of feelings, and ratings of the qualities of teams and groups. They can tally students' use of communication and conflict resolution skills, and give feedback on them. Civic organizations can help sponsor and organize Team Competitions and other performances and supply awards and certificates for performances.

Principals, superintendents, boards of education, legislators, and governors can make fundamental changes: (1) Understand how the Learn and Lose System (cf. 6) obstructs learning, (2) declare students' long-term retention of knowledge the unifying instructional principle, (3) grasp what is written above for achieving that, and (4) take it into account in decision making.

SAMPLE PERIOD

Imagine that a school recently implemented the program and a teacher invites you to observe. You enter before students arrive, and she welcomes you. "Let me show you what I'm planning," she says, and hands you the schedule:

Review practice	5 min
My presentation and discussion	15 min
Communication skills selection	1 min
Partner practice and scoring	24 min
Communication skills feedback	2 min
Mental movie	3 min
Total	50 min

"Explain it to me," you say.

"The heart of the hour is the fourth activity, practice. Students explain to partners what they just learned. For about twenty minutes they express in their own words what they got from the presentation, each one using half the time, and end knowing most or all of the lesson. From then on, periodic recall makes it permanent. First thing next class, they sink it deeper by recalling it again in review practice."

"Are they learning a lot with it?"

"We're right on track. We're aiming for a minute's worth of new knowledge every period. I usually explain a section and write it on the board. They copy it and I make sure they understand it."

"I notice two activities for communication skills," you say. "How do they fit in?"

"We integrate communications with learning. Students look at a skills sheet to select a skill to use while working with their partner. Taking a few seconds to think ahead, they're more conscious of something as simple as looking at the person who's speaking. After the practice, they get feedback from their partner, who tells them such things as 'You seemed interested in what I was saying' or noting their use of a skill. We work on communications in other ways too."

"And what's Mental Movie?"

"They close their eyes and recall everything they saw, heard, or did during the class, like watching the raw footage of a class film. Most of them have good visual memories, so this draws the whole period together. Usually two or three minutes are enough. Sometimes we use that final time for Impromptu Performance. They stand and answer questions about what they learned."

The teacher stops speaking as students walk in, and you sit down. Students look at a partner list posted by the door, find theirs, and take chairs together. Several open their notebooks and begin talking at once. When the bell rings to begin the period, the teacher says, "Please review with your partner if you haven't started." All open their notebooks and one from each pair begins talking. A student near you accepts another's notebook, asks a question from it, and scans an Answers page while listening.

The speaker says, "Ask me number fourteen. I'm not sure about that one." His partner does so, and coaches briefly while the speaker summarizes. After a couple minutes, they trade notebooks and the former listener becomes speaker. They lean toward each other, intent on what they do.

PRESENTATION

The teacher ends the review and begins a lesson about the Industrial Revolution: "The question for your Questions page is 'How did the Industrial Revolution affect workers?' She writes it at the top of the board and students copy it. As she speaks, she directs their attention to pictures in their text. She reads from Dickens's book *Hard Time*. Students close their eyes and picture it.

"Okay now, let's write out a summary of what we just covered," she says. Students then volunteer points from the presentation, she writes them on the board, and students set to work copying them: that before the Industrial Revolution, work was done by skilled craftsmen, how the use of machines put many out of work. Ned Ludd and his followers smashed machines, burned factories, and were punished and some hanged. Factory towns such as Birmingham grew four times over in fifty years and many people were homeless. *Hard Time* left images of smoke, noise, purple water, and distressed crowds of people.

With the writing done and students arranged in partners, she says, "Before you practice what we've covered, open to the communication skills and pick out one or two to use." Students open their notebooks, heads bob up and down briefly, and the teacher continues.

"Take twelve minutes each now and tell back everything you can remember that we covered. Each should be first to try half of it. If neither of you can remember a piece, refresh your memory by glancing at it, and try it again. When your partner has a chunk mastered, time their telling of it, and in their notebook under the question, mark their time and your initials."

"Can we add other stuff we read?" a student asks.

"If you've read from other books and articles, add in what you have time for. If you want, you can take notes on what your partner says to add to your own."

Another hand goes up. "I read a lot about it last night and I don't think I can tell it all back in the time I have."

"If you've outlined the answer in the Answers section of your notes as I suggested, you'll be able to hold onto it. Tell back the outline so you have the overview well in mind. On Friday we'll have a mastery review day when you can either check the timing of pieces you've already done or add new ones, so save big chunks till then to practice. Will that work for you?"

"Sure," he says.

Students exchange notebooks. The teacher assigns the first speakers to be those having first names with the earliest letter of the alphabet, and walks slowly through the classroom listening as they set to work. She returns to the board and writes three reminders about the scoring:

1. Write your partner's time under the question in their notebook beside your initials.
2. Write both of your names and scores on a slip of paper to turn in for me to post.
3. Tell your partner what skills he or she used that seemed to help you.

At ten minutes, she gets their attention and suggests that they switch if they haven't already. After twenty-two minutes, she calls time, points to the items on the board, and says, "Please complete your record-keeping and then do the feedback on skills." You see glances at the wall clock, and pencils moving in notebooks and on small slips of paper.

They turn their notebooks back to the skills list they looked at before practicing. The buzz of conversation resumes as they comment to each other. This is over in a minute, and the teacher says, "Tomorrow we'll work on the Communication Skills Check Sheet some more and do Appreciation Time. Till then, please notice the skills you see others using.

"We have a couple minutes before the bell, so could I ask everyone to do Mental Movie for the remaining time? Sit upright and comfortable, close your eyes, and try to recapture everything you learned today. Make images out of all the ideas, hear the sounds you heard, and recall your movements and feelings."

Students straighten their book bags, collect their materials, and settle in their seats. Shortly, everyone is still with eyes closed. Three minutes later when the bell rings, a few spring-loaded students are on their feet moving toward the door while others remain motionless. A minute later the last ones open their eyes, and drop their score slips into a basket on the teacher's desk as they leave.

With the teacher again, you point to a posted list titled Learning Activities and ask, "Would you explain these?"

"I've already mentioned several," she says. "We display them to remind students that they can use them to learn on their own. Present means to offer knowledge to someone else. That's mostly me, but students do it when they read a book and share it with someone else. With Understand we commit to each one understanding the first time something is presented. Sometimes their partner fills in what they didn't get from me and there are a few students I check on. In Partner Practice they retell the learning to someone else. They're also mastering nine ways to help their partner, like 'waiting while the other recalls,' 'asking partner to explain what he or she knows least,' and 'helping each other summarize answers.'

"Questions and Answers means organizing their notebooks that way. We separate them to different pages to make the notebook a better practice tool. Scoring refers to students timing or counting points of others' knowledge for a score under that question. I have their score slips now that I'll post later."

She points to a large scoreboard with names on it. "The numbers," she says, "are their scores, their daily and cumulative time and points that count up what they can explain back.

"Mental Movie we did a minute ago. With Perform, I draw a question from those they've practiced, then the name of a student to answer it. Sometimes we do these two back to back.

"CSCS means the Communication Skills Check Sheet. I asked them to look at it and pick out skills to work on during Partner Practice. Understanding Causality is a class discussion applying cause and effect to a feeling so students can tell when they are setting a feeling in motion. We've done this twice and students like it.

"Appreciation Time is powerful. After lunch they tell how others gave them good feelings or were helpful or friendly. It sounds simple but it meets their need to be validated and makes their behavior more positive. They already treat each other differently."

"What's changed most for you in this approach?" you ask.

"I hadn't realized how much time I wasted in class and how aimless they often were. The method has given me a purpose for even one spare minute. I'm better at keeping them focused."

"And your next step?" you ask.

"I'll integrate other methods gradually," she says. "Next week we'll organize the class into small groups for more student responsibility, and I'm planning a stand-up performance for parents at the end of the month."

"Would you tell the class I'm interested in their results, and will be at their performance?" you say.

"I would be delighted," she says, "and so will they."

Appendix 1

Feelings List

adequate
affectionate
alert
alone
ambitious
angry
anxious
apathetic
apologetic
appreciated
assured
awed
awkward
bad
belonging
bored
close
competent
concerned
contented
controlling
dependent
desire for attention
depressed
determined
disappointed
distant
down
ecstatic
edgy
embarrassed
empty
energetic
enthusiastic
envious
excited
fearful
flowing
focused
free
friendly
frustrated
good
gracious
grieved
guilty
happy
hassled
hated
hopeful
helpless
hurt
inadequate
independent
indignant
inferior
insecure
involved
irritated
jealous
joyful
left out
lonely
lost
loved
loving
masterful
mistrusting
needed
neglected
neutral
non-involved
nostalgic
optimistic
pessimistic
possessive
powerful
protective
proud
put down
rebellious
regretful
rejected
rejecting
relaxed
relieved
remorseful
resentful
respectful
responsible
sad
secure

self-blaming
self-conscious
serene
silly
shamed
shy
"small" feeling
sorry for self
spaced out
stressed
stubborn
superior
threatened
tired
tolerant
tranquil
troubled
trusting
uneasy
unneeded
unwanted
up
valuable
wanted
weak
weary
willful
wonder
worried
worthless
wronged

Appendix 2

First Grade Topics

One first grade class listed the following topics they would like to talk about:

animals	plants	swimming	Christmas
food	school rules	puppets	zoo
families	how to be good	world	jokes
cartoons	songs	things we learn	rhymes
video games	P.E.	music	alphabet
TV shows	centers in the room	homework	birds
games	fruits	helping at home	computers
dinosaurs	coloring books	recess	extinct animal
places to go	colors	fish	trees
mall	washing	fishing	insects
shopping	movies	hunting	sports
school	playing with friends	Halloween	sports players
favorite books	numbers	Mother's Day	authors
restaurants	camping	meats	ice cream
eating with family		teachers	class field trips
cleaning the school		parks	flowers

Appendix 3

Fourth Grade Topics

A fourth grade class listed the following topics they would like to talk about:

basketball	football	soccer	baseball
sportswear	Indians	gangs	weather
gas	money	volcano	girls
boys	cats	clothes	fighting
principal	trees	homework	tap dance
dentist	games	wolves	kickball
aliens	hair	wrestling	free time
bears	body	boxing	

Appendix 4

Issues for Middle and High School Students

when I was close to danger
when I wanted to be free
depending on others
accidents
pressure from parents
pressure from teachers
pressure from peers
family differences
being a parent
I'd like to be able to . . .
Giving and receiving compliments
having my own family
feelings parents give you
the future
feelings from girls
feelings from boys
being a male
being a female

if I could . . .
how I would . . .
feelings from money
creating my own feelings
groups I've been in
groups I've been outside of
law
fighting
how I listen
loss I've experienced
fear of death
being around death
controlling myself
controlling others
being controlled
saying goodbye
being guessed about
guessing about others

what I think I need
discounts and putdowns
asking for help
being on my own
feelings different from others
what I like about me physically
pain
my experience being liked
my experience being disliked
what I'm good at
what gives me good feelings
what I want to be good at
a wild idea I had
what others may not like about me
having to lead
how my moods change
being looked at by others
getting poor grades

being made fun of	liking someone	facing a teacher
racial discrimination	communicating when it's hard	facing a principal
authority	experiences with power	performing
feelings about how I look	experiences with truth	fear of not succeeding
being picked on	experiences with a neighbor	wondering if I'm ready to graduate
being on a team	experiences with a friend	things I'm not ready for
resolutions I've made	experiences with work	how I see myself in the future
troubles I've had	experiences with lying	when others encroach on me
facing a fight	how I finish what I start	when I encroach on others
my parents' generation	organizing myself	promises to myself
feelings about sports	mixed feelings about things	promises to others
family relationships	wishing for things	worries about being fat/thin
speaking in class	wondering what's real	worries about my complexion/hair
drugs and alcohol	knowing an opportunity	worries about my clothes
smoking	hiding feelings	

Appendix 5

Advanced Topics

ability
acceptance
accusation
acquiring
advice
agreement
alcohol
ancestry
anger
animals
annoyances
approval
attention
beauty
begging
beginning
belief
books
boredom
brother
calmness
care
causation
certainty
chance
change
character
charity
cheerfulness
children
choice
cleanness
cleverness
clumsiness
command
complaint
concealment
confusion
congratulations
contempt
consensus
control
cooperation
courage
courtesy
cruelty
cure
dance
darkness
death
debt
deception
decision
defeat
defiance
departure
desertion
desire
destiny
difficulty
disagreement
disappointment
discovery
disobedience
disrespect
dissatisfaction
divorce
drama
drink
drugs
duty
ease
economy
elders
elegance
elimination
embarrassment
encroachment
enthusiasm
equality
evening
exaggeration
examination
excitement
exclusion
expectation
failure
fame
family
fashion
father
fatigue

fear
feeling
female
fighter
fine arts
follower
folly
food
foresight
forgetfulness
forgiveness
freedom
friend
future
ghost
giving
government
gratitude
greatness
greed
guilt
habit
hair
happiness
harm
hatred
head
health
heaven
height
hindsight
hitting
home
honesty
hope
humility
humiliation
ignorance
illegality
imagination
imitation
immorality
importance
imprisonment
inferiority
influence
insanity
insensitivity
institutions
intelligence
intuition
killing
kindness
land
law
leader
life
light
liking
loss
love
loyalty
luck
marriage
maturity
meddling
mementos
messes
milestone
miscalculations
misinterpretation
money
morality
morning
mother
motivation
mountain
mystery
names
naturalness
necessity
neighbor
nervousness
nobility
obvious
offer
official
oldness
opening
opinion
opposition
ostentation
ownership
pain
passage
past
patriotism
payment
peace
perfection
permission
persuasion
pity
plan
playfulness
pleasure
possibility
power
poverty
prejudice
preparation
pressure
pretense
pride
privilege
privacy
promise
protection
punishment
purpose
rank
receiving
rejection
relationship
relatives
relief
respect
rest
restraint
risk
roles
room
routine
rules
sale
sanity
school
scolding
seasons
selfishness
sensitiveness
sentimentality
service
severity
sex
similarity
simplicity
sister

size	sufficiency	touch	vision
sleep	suggestion	travel	voice
slowness	suicide	truth	war
sobriety	superiority	unbelief	warning
sociality	support	uncertainty	waste
space	surprise	understanding	weakness
speed	taking	unfairness	will
spirituality	talk	uniformity	wisdom
strength	taste	universe	work
stubbornness	teaching	unreal	world
stupidity	tendency	unreasonableness	you
submission	thought	unselfishness	
success	threat	unusualness	
suddenness	time	value	

Appendix 6

Blank Chart

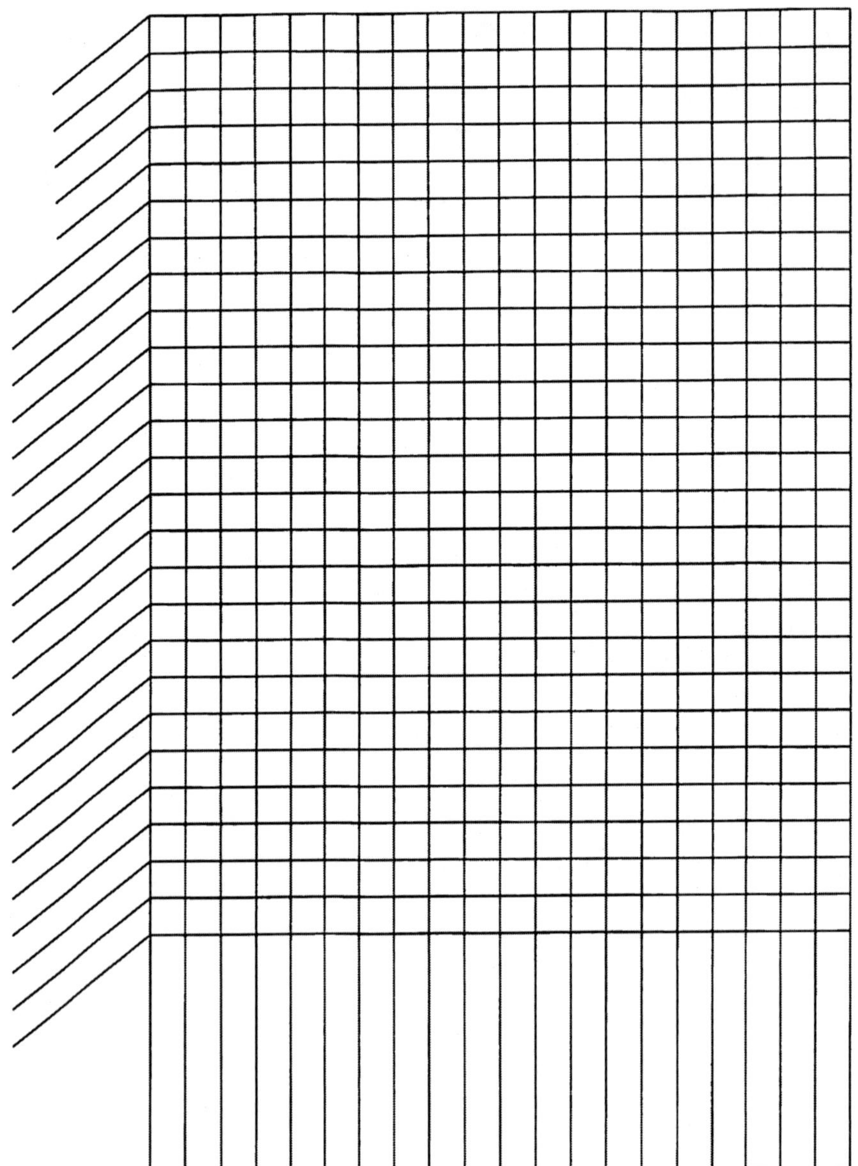

Appendix 7

Points and Mastery Scoreboards

POINTS SCOREBOARD

Name	Monday	Tuesday	Wednesday	Thursday	Friday	Cumulative

MASTERY SCOREBOARD

Name	TIME Daily	TIME Total	POINTS Daily	POINTS Total	COMBINED TOTAL

Appendix 8

Progress Ladder

Progress Ladder

Each column is used for rating yourself on one day a week. Write the rating date at the top of the column. Draw a bar across the column at the level your progress reached in that rating period.

Date												
Winners. Know what they want and act toward that steadily. They practice new habits and develop new skills constantly. They are willing to work at odd times, can sacrifice recreation for study or work. Will work at their goals while others play. Can face opposition and keep going steadily all day. Will work even when tired. Can face discouragement and get self "up" again. They feel valuable (able to create value), give others good feelings steadily, and enjoy drawing out others' best. Habitually considerate and acceptant toward all.												
Contenders. Some periodic enthusiasm gets person up and going. Can work hard but sometimes quits soon. Has goals but loses track of them frequently. Not willing to work when others play. Won't make sacrifices to achieve goals. Practices skills intermittently. Confident in some areas. Willing to be courteous, but only gives good feelings to those who return them. Lets circumstances become stronger than his/her own choices.												
Entrants. Is interested in doing better, but doesn't understand that this requires setting some things aside. Needs coaching and encouragement, but doesn't ask for it. Tends to drift. Will practice skills and develop knowledge if directed to do so, and will work while it's enjoyable. Depends on others to plan for him/her. Will help others when asked, but is more concerned with how others treat him/her than how he/she is treating others. Goals are more in the form of wishes.												
Undecided. The undecided is basically waiting, hoping something will turn up. The best he/she can do is wait in the presence of others who are doing better, and watch them, listen, look, and think. From this beginning, the undecided can learn to follow directions, and begin to think and work toward personal goals. Currently works only when inclined to, when there is nothing else to do. Is easily distracted by others and will set aside goals for TV, conversation, or old habits. Expects to succeed without any personal change. Is absorbed in own feelings and finds it difficult to give others sustained attention.												

Appendix 9

Communication Skills Check Sheet

Communication Skills Check Sheet

Each vertical column is for checking one experience. Go down one column (for example, column 1) and put in the rating on each skill for the person you observed:

0 = didn't use this one at all
1 = used it but poorly
2 = used it moderately well
3 = used it very well, or frequently, or very appropriately

Name ______	1	2	3	4	5	6	7	8	9	10	11	12	13
1. CHECK YOUR INNER ACTIVITY													
a. Notice others' desire to speak.													
b. Feel respect and consideration.													
c. Focus on the one speaking.													
d. Wait while the other finishes.													
e. Then share your ideas and feelings.													
2. LISTEN TO WHOEVER IS TALKING													
a. Look at speaker.													
b. Don't interrupt. Say "Excuse me" if you do.													
c. Ask speaker to continue.													
d. Leave brief silence when speaker ends.													
3. INCLUDE EVERYONE													
a. Invite those to talk who haven't.													
b. Give equal time talking.													
c. Ask questions and accept answers.													
f. Use others' names.													
4. GIVE A GOOD FEELING													
a. Take interest in what others say.													
b. Ask about their feelings and accept them.													
d. Thank people.													
e. Give compliments.													
f. Tell what helped you.													
5. CONNECT TO WHAT OTHERS SAY													
a. Remember what others say.													
b. Use others' words and ideas.													
c. Note similarity or differences compared to your ideas.													
d. Describe what affects you.													
e. Check guesses about others' thoughts and feelings.													
f. Summarize others' thoughts and feelings.													
g. Talk out problems.													
TOTAL SCORE													

Appendix 10

Individual Match Worksheet

Meet location ________________
Date ________________
Judge ________________
Point Student __________Team __________
Questioner__________Team__________

1. Total mastery knowledge claimed by point student:

____

1 Question #	2 Time/Pts Claimed	3 Bonus % Added	4 Deficit% Taken	5 Time/Pts Verified
1				
2				
3				
4				
5				
6				
7				
8				
9				
10				
11				
12				
13				
14				
15				
16				
17				
18				
19				
20				
Totals				

2. Question time credited (total of column 5) divided by question time claimed (total of column 2) = percent of mastery time credited________________.
3. Total mastery knowledge claimed (line 1 above)________________ × percent mastery time credited (line 2 above)________________ = total mastered knowledge verified________________.
4. If line 1 is greater than line 3, then total mastery knowledge claimed (line 1) minus total mastery knowledge verified (line 3) = award to opposing team________________, subtracted from the score of the point student's team on scoreboard and added to opposing team's score.
5. If line 1 is smaller than line 3, then total mastery knowledge verified (line 3) minus total mastery knowledge claimed (line 1) = award to point student's team________________, added to its score on scoreboard.

WORKSHEET INSTRUCTIONS

An individual match is a question-answer exchange between a point student and a questioner. A separate worksheet is made out for each individual match. A student's amount of claimed learning is judged during questioning to be stronger or weaker than claimed. If weaker, the increment is subtracted from his or her own team's total and added to the opposing team's; if stronger, it is added to his or her own team's total. To determine this accurately, a judge weighs the student's claim question by question as the match proceeds.

Afterward, the scoring team combines the judge's assessment of individual questions into a single percent that reflects the overall strength or weakness of the student's knowledge and applies this to the knowledge claimed, adding the plus increment to the student's team score or subtracting a minus increment from his or her team score and adding it to the other team's.

Students may score some of their knowledge as time and some as points. To make the scoring comparable for competition, organizers need to agree on which to use and then convert all scores to that one. In general, the younger the students, the more easily they'll use points and the older they are, the more likely time is preferred. The former are best for concrete, factual knowledge and the latter for synthesizing ideas. To convert points into time, divide the number of points by four (e.g., eight points divided by four = 2) and add the result to the total time (= add 2 minutes to time total). To go the other way and convert time into points, multiply minutes (with seconds expressed as a decimal) by four and add the result to the total points (e.g., 2 minutes and 30 seconds = 2.50 × 4 = 10 = add 10 points to the point total).

For rapid addition of times or their conversion to points, express seconds as the nearest quarter-minute so that each 15 seconds equals one point. Thus 1 minute and 20 seconds is closer to 1 minute and 15 than to 1 minute and 30, so as a decimal it's counted as a minute and a quarter, or 1.25 minutes, or 5 points. Thus 1:40 is closer to 1:45, so it equals 1.75 minutes or 7 points.

1. *Scoring team preparations.* The scoring team prepares for the competition and assists the judges and participants.

    a) They record on a scoreboard visible to everyone the initial Total Team Challenge (TTC) of each team. One design for it is a large dry erase board positioned vertically with a line down the middle. One team's TTC is entered at the top of one column and the other team's at the top of the other. As new scores are added and subtracted below it, spectators can follow the changes in scoring round by round.
    b) On the worksheet for each individual match, the scoring team enters the names of the judge, point student, questioner, and their team names; and on line 1 the amount of mastered knowledge the point student claims (as points or time, whichever is selected by the organizers). They hand the worksheet to the judge along with the point student's backup material when the judge is ready to begin the turn.

2. *Judge conducts the questioning.* The judge receives the worksheet for that turn from the scorers.

    a) When the participants are ready, the judge starts a timing device. The questioner locates the answer in the point student's material by giving a page and answer-number reference to the judge, and asks the first question of the point student.
    b) The judge records in column one the answer-number that identifies its location in the student's material, and in column two the time (or points) the student claims for it. He or she then listens to the point student's answer, comparing it to the answer the student claimed to know.
    c) When the student's answer for that question is complete, the judge determines whether the student actually knew more or less than the amount claimed. He or she assigns either a bonus or deficit, or validates the amount as claimed, and enters the result in columns to the right; a bonus in column three as a plus percent (e.g., + 3%) or a deficit in column four as a minus percent (e.g., – 7%). If the judge validates that what was claimed was known, then he or she draws a line through columns three and four indicating to the scoring team that no adjustment was needed in the amount claimed.

d) The point student answers as many questions as time allows and the judge fills in the first four columns for each question as appropriate. When that student's time is up, the judge completes the notations, hands the worksheet to the scoring team, and prepares for another individual match.

3. *Scoring team completes the scoring.* The scoring team receives worksheets for each round from the judge, completes them, and converts the judge's ratings into an amount of increase or decrease of the team TTC score and records it on the scoreboard as follows:

   a) For each question listed, they convert the judge's adjustment into a full percentage figure. If the judge gave a bonus of 3% for a particular question, they enter 103% in column three beside the judge's notation, and if the judge gave a deficit of 7% on another question, they enter a 93% figure in column four beside the judge's figure.
   b) For each question, they then multiply the percentage figures (containing the bonus from column three or deficit from column four) times the score claimed for that question in column two, and record the result in column five for each question. They carry the multiplication out to two decimal places in order to register the difference between percentages assigned.
   c) When all questions are scored individually, the scoring team obtains a total for column two and a total for column five. They divide the latter by the former to obtain the overall percent of all the questions validated or credited (compared to the amount claimed for those specific questions). They record the final percent on line two below the worksheet.
   d) Next they compare this to the student's total, claimed body of knowledge. For this (following the blanks in line three), they multiply the total claimed knowledge from line one (first blank) times the percent entered on line two (second blank) to obtain the total verified knowledge and they record the product (third blank).
   e) The scoring team determines the difference between the claimed score (line one) and the verified score (line three, last blank) obtained in the prior step. The smaller is subtracted from the larger.
   f) If the verified score is lower than the claimed score (because of deficits assigned by the judge), the verified score is subtracted from the claimed score (line four). The difference is subtracted from his or her team's score on the scoreboard and added to the opposing team's score on the scoreboard.

g) If the verified score is the higher amount (because of bonuses awarded for questions by the judge), the scoring team subtracts the claimed score from the verified score. The difference is added to the point student's team score on the scoreboard (line five).

h) If the verified and claimed scores are the same (because the student successfully defended 100% mastery of his claimed knowledge) his or her team's score remains unchanged on the scoreboard.

Notes

1. "Brain Imaging Identifies Best Memorization Strategies," Brenda Kirchhoff and Randy L. Buckner, *Science Daily*, August 10, 2006. Researchers at Washington University in St. Louis found that the memory strategies of visualizing carefully what was to be remembered and constructing sentences about the objects to remember were the best of several attempted (citing the July 20, 2006 issue of *Neuron*).
2. "Testing Strengthens Recall Whether Something's on the Test or Not," APA Press Release, November 12, 2006. Researchers found that just taking a test helps students remember everything they learned. Summarizes "Retrieval-Induced Facilitation: Initially Nontested Material Can Benefit From Prior Testing of Related Material," Jason C. K. Chan, Kathleen B. McDermott, and Henry L. Roediger, *Journal of Experimental Psychology*: General, Vol. 135, No. 4 (November 2006 issue). Authors note that this supports teachers' practice of regularly giving essay or short-answer exams that call up related or extraneous information: "This sort of all-inclusive retrieval strategy might be beneficial to retention in the long run."
3. *Pygmalion in the Classroom*, Robert Rosenthal and Lenore Jacobsen (Holt, Rinehart, and Winston: New York, 1968). This classic study illuminates the power of teacher belief. Many teachers actually preferred students staying as they were. Those labeled as poor learners got the most flack from teachers when they "stepped out of character" with improved results, even though it was the teachers' own grudging expectations that appeared to generate the results.
4. "Friendly Persuasion," James M. Kauffman et al., *Human Behavior*, September 1977.
5. If someone expresses a crudity about the word feeling when you start Appreciation Time, take it as an implied need. Ignore it at first, but if it is repeated, ask them "Are you uncomfortable with that word?" They may be, but try it anyway because it's the easiest to use: "We want to use words accurately, and that one tells what we mean, but if you need to, we can use a different one like, 'Who caused you to feel better?' or 'Who gave you a positive emotion?' Do you understand 'positive emotion'? Or we could say, 'Who was friendly to you?' Do you think you would be more comfortable with that?" Speak with a solicitous voice. You convey seriousness by insisting on using words accurately. An expert high school teacher focuses on the precise meaning of words to handle inappropriate comments from students. Before they begin, they know "I'm not going to get around this lady," and give up distractive comments.
6. *Naikan: Gratitude, Grace, and the Japanese Art of Self-Reflection*, Gregg Krech (Stone Bridge Press: Berkeley, 2002). Krech describes a philosophy of life and healing based on gratitude for all that is given us. Contains many exercises a teacher could readily apply to the classroom for stretching students' awareness and attitudes.

7. A discussion about how to describe a skill in either positive or negative terms may expand their understanding. On the Communication Skills Check Sheet, both forms are present; the affirmative in 1d and 1e, and the negative in 2b. From kindergarten on, children know the meaning of "Don't interrupt" because the negative form has been used so much more than the positive but discussing it in both forms generates better understanding.
8. This stripped-down set of five steps was developed in Alaska's Juneau/Douglas School District. Its brevity makes it handy for student use.
9. *Emotional Intelligence: Why It Can Matter More Than IQ*, Daniel Goleman (Bantam Books: New York, 1995). Goleman devotes Chapter 6 to "The Master Aptitude," the ability to regulate our moods. The entire book explores different facets of emotional self-management. Its explanation of how emotion "hijacks" thinking could help many teachers.
10. Be aware of how your terminology translates to students. Most may understand that "bad" feelings are "unpleasant, sad, or unhappy," but some may code the term as "blameworthy." To make sure everyone understands your words the same way, you may need to explain them when you first use them.
11. *Health Dispatch*, Dr. David Williams, December 2003. Cites researchers at the Karolinska Hospital in Sweden who discovered that humming increases air exchange in the sinus cavities, helping them produce nitric oxide, which in turn helps dilate capillary beds and increase blood flow. During humming, nitric oxide levels appear to be 15 times higher than during normal breathing and the gas exchange between the nasal passages and the sinuses was 98% in one exhalation, almost a complete exchange whereas 4% is normal. This matters because poor gas exchange and circulation in the sinus cavities make bacterial growth and infection easier. Researchers feel that daily breathing exercises involving humming could help reduce the incidence of sinusitis and upper respiratory infections. Done for long periods, this is likely to lead to increased mental clarity by increasing blood flow and oxygenation in the brain and may alleviate chronic sinus problems (Am J Respir Crit Care Med 02;166(2):131–2).
12. The concept of a resource state has been developed in numerous books by John Grinder and Richard Bandler as part of a therapeutic approach called Neuro-Linguistic Programming (NLP). Cf. *Trance-Formations* and *Frogs into Princes*, both by John Grinder and Richard Bandler (Real People Press, Moab, Utah, 1979). Most development involves obtaining greater access to resource states or creating them where they are missing. The process described is a way to restore people to their personal strengths. Extensive applications of these ideas are available by searching "neuro-linguistic programming."
13. Said to be the basis of most civil law, these questions are taken from *Whatever Happened to Justice?*, Richard Maybury (Bluestocking Press: Shingle Springs, CA, 1990).
14. These two questions, a constructive stance to all interactions, are the basis of the ECK Neighbor Program.
15. "Optimization Versus Effortful Processing in Children: Cognitive Triage: Criticisms, Reanalyses, and New Data," C. J. Brainerd et al., *Journal of Experimental Child Psychology*, Vol. 55, No. 3, pp. 353–73, June 1993.
16. *The Tipping Point: How Little Things Can Make a Big Difference*, Malcolm Gladwell (Little, Brown and Company: New York, 2000). Gladwell explains the psychology behind the Broken Windows theory, that correcting small misbehaviors diminishes large misbehaviors that would occur otherwise. Its outcomes in New York City offer many parallels for application to schools.
17. Classroom rules can occasion a discussion of values and choices. Teachers in your school may suggest what has worked with students like yours. In different classrooms one encounters many different rule sets such as the following, which invites a thoughtful stance toward the system, physical objects, and people: (1) Do your best. (2) Don't interfere. Allow others to do their best. (3) Follow all lawful directives of staff the first time. (4) Don't divert the class. Solve problems outside class. (5) Respect private and public property. (6) Be considerate to all others in and outside of class. Make it a Learning Feat everyone masters perfectly.
18. *The New York Times*, "Bad habits? My future self will deal with that," Alina Tugend, February 24, 2012.

19. For more on using the imagination, see Chapter 8. Practice With the Imagination, in *Changing Attitudes and Behavior: Practice Makes Permanent*.
20. "Cooperative Learning in Dyads," Celia O. Larson, *Journal of Reading*, Vol. 29, No. 6, pp. 516–20 (March 1986).
21. See tprsource.com
22. The source was a journal printed probably in the 1950s or1960s that has eluded my attempts to track it down.
23. See reference 1.
24. "Sleep to Remember," Matthew P. Walker, *American Scientist*, July–August 2006. Summarizes the forms of memory and how practice, rehearsal, and sleep are connected. Sleep is important in consolidating memory, and adequate sleep is especially necessary to prepare the brain to receive and sustain new memory.
25. The three-step "universal success formula" proposed by Richard Bandler and John Grinder is useful knowledge to pass on to students: well-formed goals (so you have direction), sensory acuity (so you know whether you are getting there), and behavioral flexibility (so you can change your effort to get better results). See reference 12.
26. "Novelty Aids Learning," *Eurekalert*, August 3, 2006, summarizing an article published in *Neuron* August 3, 2006.
27. *What Smart Students Know: Maximum Grades, Optimum Learning, Minimum Time*, Adam Robinson (Random House: New York, 1993). Robinson explains why reorganizing and summarizing is a valuable means of retaining knowledge.
28. Principals and trainers can encounter a focus on mistakes that they would like to change. A spelling test can help teachers appreciate the effect of their attitude on students. Introduce it early on a training day: "I'd like to assign people to the next exercises today based on how well you do on this first one, a spelling test for college freshmen." With a straight face, dictate the following for them to spell: asinine, braggadocio, accommodate, diarrhea, chauffeur, desiccate, impostor, inoculate, hors d'oeuvres, liquefy, mayonnaise, moccasin, obbligato, narcissistically, rococo, benefited, rarefy, resuscitate, sacrilegious, supersede, titillate, and paraphernalia. They exchange papers. You then spell the words correctly while they place an X beside the wrong answers on the paper they have. They write the number incorrect at the top and return it. You list a column of numbers on the board from zero down to twenty, and then check how many got each number of mistakes: "How many got zero mistakes?" "How many got one wrong?" They raise their hand at their number of mistakes. You count up the hands raised and note it beside that number. When all scores are noted, ask them how they feel. Though typically generating laughter, it also carries them back to how children may feel about a focus on their mistakes. In small groups, they might discuss how the spelling test experience could relate to their instructional approach.
29. "Rutgers-Newark Researcher: Brains of Dyslexic Children can be 'Rewired' to Improve Reading Skills," Rutgers-Newark News Service, March 4, 2003, and "Dyslexics Not Doomed to Life of Reading Difficulties," Joel Schwarz, University of Washington, February 13, 2004. Studies from different sources are finding that teaching dyslexics by means of the links between sound, letters, and meaning can dramatically improve their reading.
30. If I'm a parent receiving my child's report and see an A, a B, and a C, what do they mean? I don't know because they are not linked to any stable reference point but rather reflect the teacher comparing him with others, often giving a false picture. A B in one school may equal D in another, grade inflation is endemic, grades can be assigned to pacify parents and not jar students, physical presence or verbal participation matter more to some teachers than to others, unconscious beliefs about status and racial bias can skew grades, tests for one demographic may be unfair to others, and teachers may want to "send a message." Courses in how to take tests distort the meaning of differences in scores, teaching to the test can cause an overall decrease in learning, and grading on the curve removes it from a direct relationship to the student's own effort.
31. For students raised under cultural norms that young people should remain silent, mention to them that a classroom differs from being in the presence of elders. All their lives they will need to grasp the standards of the setting they are in ("When in Rome . . ."). In school, they develop knowledge by expressing it.

32. "How We Know: What Do an Algebra Teacher, Toyota, and a Classical Musician Have in Common?" Jonah Lehrer, *Seed*, September 2006, pp. 70–73. Lehrer notes Ericsson's finding that peak performers practice differently than others. They do fewer mindless drills and less rote repetition but make sessions deliberate, creative, and thoughtful. They set goals, analyze their progress steadily, and focus on their process of learning, always integrating learning with their doing.
33. "The many health perks of good handwriting: Not only does it help the brain develop, it can also improve grades and confidence," Julie Deardorff, *Los Angeles Times*, June 11, 2011. Writing is especially critical at the very beginning. Children learn letters and number rapidly when writing them is a large part of their learning.
34. "Film Shows How Teams Bring Out Best in People," Doug Wallace, *Minneapolis Star Tribune*, April 10, 1995, p. 2D.